English for Academic Purp

CRITICAL NEW LITERACIES: THE PRAXIS OF ENGLISH LANGUAGE TEACHING AND LEARNING (PELT)

Volume 2

Series Editors:

Marcelle Cacciattolo, *Victoria University, Australia*
Tarquam McKenna, *Victoria University, Australia*
Shirley Steinberg, *University of Calgary, Canada*
Mark Vicars, *Victoria University, Australia*

As a praxis-based sequence these texts are specifically designed by the team of international scholars to engage in local in-country language pedagogy research. This exciting and innovative series will bring a dynamic contribution to the development of critical new literacies. With a focus on literacy teaching, research methods and critical pedagogy, the founding principle of the series is to investigate the practice of new literacies in English language learning and teaching, as negotiated with relevance to the localized educational context. It is being and working alongside people in the world that is at the core of the PELT viewpoint. The Praxis of English Language Teaching and Learning series will focus on inter-culturality and interdisciplinary qualitative inquiry and the dissemination of "non-colonised" research.

English for Academic Purposes (EAP) in Asia

Negotiating Appropriate Practices in a Global Context

Edited by

Indika Liyanage
Tony Walker
Griffith University, Australia

SENSE PUBLISHERS
ROTTERDAM / BOSTON / TAIPEI

A C.I.P. record for this book is available from the Library of Congress.

ISBN 978-94-6209-750-6 (paperback)
ISBN 978-94-6209-751-3 (hardback)
ISBN 978-94-6209-752-0 (e-book)

Published by: Sense Publishers,
P.O. Box 21858, 3001 AW Rotterdam, The Netherlands
https://www.sensepublishers.com/

Printed on acid-free paper

To

The late Dr Gary John Birch
Principal Supervisor of our Doctorates

and

Mithila & Megan

TABLE OF CONTENTS

PREFACE

It is widely acknowledged that academic practices of learning and constructing knowledge are locally negotiated and constituted. In the contemporary global linguistic landscape, English is increasingly replacing local languages as the medium of instruction (MOI) in schools and Universities in Asia. This has, more than ever, necessitated the provision of English for Academic Purposes (EAP) as an integral element of education in this region. However, the skills and practices required for learning and negotiating cognitively demanding academic tasks embedded in the EAP delivered to students in local contexts tend to be those used in Western English-speaking contexts rather than those indigenous to local academic communities of practice. This conflation of the English language and the practices of English-speaking academia in non-Anglophone academic settings assumes an inherent superiority of such practices of learning and engagement in academic activities. Tensions between diverse academic conventions and practices are also increasingly demanding attention in academic contexts in English-speaking countries that traditionally served the needs of monolingual domestic cohorts of students using elite Western varieties of English and EAP practices. Internationalization of higher education in English-speaking nations has brought about profound changes in demographic characteristics of student populations; despite increased participation rates of foreign students, especially from Asian countries, the academic practices these students bring with them are in most cases deemed inadequate and inappropriate for success in a setting where superiority of practices of English-speaking academia continues to be assumed.

This volume, however, is not a collection of ideas to highlight linguistic or academic imperialism in Asian educational contexts. It is rather an attempt to explore the interface of language and academic practices and how this can be negotiated to generate locally informed and situated academic approaches. Although other works have directed attention to EAP instruction as it is practised in the West and in preparation of students for overseas study, little has been written about teaching of EAP from the perspectives of Asian practitioners who prepare students for education through the English medium in local schools and universities or who face various contextual struggles and difficulties. Even scantier attention has been given to how Asian EAP practices are perceived within academic programs in English-speaking countries by academics.

Our focus specifically is to explore ways in which EAP practitioners negotiate the implementation of locally situated academic practices in the provision of EAP, and how these are accommodated within academic programs in educational establishments in English-speaking countries. In particular, we highlight the tensions involved in implementing EAP programs across a varied platform of settings (schools, technical colleges, universities, and private institutions) in Asia. In doing so, we foreground perspectives of local practitioners who negotiate these tensions from a selection of Asian EAP contexts (i.e., Sri Lanka, China, Nepal,

Bangladesh & Pakistan), and an English-speaking county in Australasia – Australia.

The book therefore offers fresh perspectives by academics of EAP contexts they represent; the chapters draw on original research, or focus on emerging and contemporary views of EAP in their contexts. The specific concerns the authors of these chapters voice are not only relevant to countries these authors represent. They are relevant to the entire Asian region and, by extension, to other non-English-speaking countries where EAP instruction is common. The audience for this book are those researchers, practitioners, and postgraduate students who have developmental and operational concerns of EAP in Asia as well as those involved in EAP practices in other contexts. Those with broader interests in areas such as emerging paradigms for English-language teaching and learning, higher education policy issues, settings characterized by multilingual and plurilingual communities, internationalization of higher education, or the role of critical thinking will also find the work presented here of value.

We would like to acknowledge and thank colleagues who acted as anonymous reviewers for chapters in this book: Radhika De Silva (Open University of Sri Lanka), Adriana Diaz (Griffith University, Australia), Ben Fenton-Smith (Griffith University, Australia), Mufeeda Irshad (University of Groningen, Nethelands), Kerryn McCluskey (University of Queensland, Australia), Susan Bridges (Hong Kong University), and Vivimarie Vanderpoorten (Open University of Sri Lanka). Also, we extend our gratitude for the support of Sense Publishers including Michel Lokhorst and Bernice Kelly.

Indika Liyanage and Tony Walker
January 2014

INDIKA LIYANAGE & TONY WALKER

1. ACCOMMODATING ASIAN EAP PRACTICES WITHIN POSTGRADUATE TEACHER EDUCATION

Perspectives from Australia

INTRODUCTION

A powerful discourse in the contemporary world connects the dominance of the West and education. Perceptions of educational standards and institutions of the English-speaking West as superior have synonymized a Western education with opportunities to achieve aspirations of economic growth and prosperity (Gray, 2010). Towards the close of the 20th century, there were more than a million students in higher education worldwide who were studying outside their own countries (Huxur, Mansfield, Nnazor, Schuetze, & Segawa, 1996), a figure that increases every year as international students comprise an expanding component of student enrolments, particularly in Western universities. In Australian postgraduate coursework programs in 2010, for example, 47% of total equivalent full-time student load were international students, predominantly from nations in Asia (Department of Education Employment and Workplace Relations, 2011). The number of students studying outside their home country is predicted to grow to 7 million by 2025 (Ruby, 2008), the majority from non-English-speaking backgrounds (NESB) and studying in the English-speaking nexus of Britain, Australasia, and North America (BANA). Integral to successful participation in Western education is mastery of its language of instruction, a prestige variety of English, and of inherent academic practices and conventions. Coupled with other powerful socio-political forces, these perceptions have generated concomitant diminution in perceptions of the socio-educational value of local languages, including non-prestige varieties of English, and of local/indigenous academic practices and conventions. Rapid increases in the population aspiring to learn English as a Second or Foreign Language (ESL/EFL) in order to study in Western institutions (Birch & Liyanage, 2004) have sparked an ongoing worldwide increase in demand for English for Academic Purposes (EAP) courses varying in length and the mode of instruction (Jordan, 1997) to prepare students to study in English-speaking academia.

International postgraduate students from Asia who have successfully completed an EAP course can discover, however, that pursuit of academic achievement and success in postgraduate teacher education programs (PTEPs) in Australia is complicated by their use of diverse Englishes. Current thinking about varieties of English, the English as an International Language (EIL) paradigm, assumes that English does not belong to any particular language community, shifting attention to

I. Liyanage & T. Walker (eds.), English for Academic Purposes (EAP) in Asia, 1–12.

accommodation and mutual intelligibility in intercultural interactions in which English is used. Although a significant hallmark of the spread of English outside BANA nations has been its appropriation by users in other contexts (Canagarajah, 1999), in the EAP context varieties of English other than that demanded by the conventions of Western academia "are used to exclude many of its users, to construct an inferior" (Phan, 2007, p. 48). EAP presents as the target variety of academic English one which is considered by Westerners, by virtue of a perceived epistemological universality, to be culturally neutral but which, in reality, represents a preferred variety of English that has embedded in it Western ways of learning and Western ways of organizing and generating knowledge. At the level of target variety of English, EAP encompasses not just the mechanics of language and accurate use; what is involved includes aspects of language use that are bound up, not with English proficiency, but with cultural communication styles (Fox, 1994; Phan, 2011). Although we can accept representation of the linguistic resources and discursive practices presented through EAP and associated materials as tools for mediation of content knowledge, they serve to achieve much more, as powerful tools for the reproduction of ideologies and of a particular way of constructing reality (Gray, 2010). International students from nations outside the English-speaking BANA countries, but where English is a medium of instruction (MOI), are accomplished users of varieties and academic practices that are considered educated in their local contexts of origin. Many of these students, for example, some participants in Phan's (2011) study of Vietnamese postgraduates studying in Australia, are graduates, often with distinction, of programs in which their local variety of English is the MOI. Other international students have engaged in the study of the English language for the express purpose of studying at a university in an English-speaking country. As postgraduates, these students can also point to prior academic success, but in a language other than English. Yet another group are recent immigrants from Asian nations, of diverse linguistic profiles, returning to study as domestic student enrolments.

Many international students for whom Australian English is not their first language struggle with the language demands of their studies, not only in PTEPs, and can "suffer an academic dissonance and a sense of academic shock when they are not able to achieve at the high levels they are accustomed to at home" (Spooner-Lane, Tangen, & Campbell, 2009, p. 81), and can face failure, despite meeting language requirements (Coley, 1999; Hawthorne, Minas, & Singh, 2004). A study of English language entry requirements of 37 Australian universities (Coley, 1999) concluded that it was possible for students who have satisfied the requirements to subsequently be considered inept. Significant numbers of international students report experiencing a range of language difficulties in academic situations (see Dunworth & Kirkpatrick, 2003; Liddicoat, 2003; Liyanage & Birch, 2001; Walker, 2010). Similar reports are given by students in studies of cultural and linguistic diversity among domestic students (for example, Asmar, 2005; Borland & Pearce, 2002; Chanock & Cargill, 2003; Wilson, 2003).

Current Approaches

Linguistic and cultural difference has been historically associated in the Australian higher education sector with necessity to provide language and learning support (Asmar, 2005). Responses, and research, have taken two predominant approaches. One, the "deficit" approach, rejects tolerance for diversity and instead acknowledges and accepts privileging of particular discourses of the English-speaking academy (Altbach, 2004; Koehne, 2004) in Australian institutions, ascribes any mismatch between teachers' expectations and students' performances to the students, and advocates remediation, adjustment, and adaptation on the part of students. This model sees students identified as requiring support directed to language and learning support services or discrete language enrichment courses. There has been a focus on researching the teaching of academic skills, primarily academic writing, and the training and support of students to enable participation and the completion of academic tasks (see for example, Clerehan, 2004; Cruickshank, Newell, & Cole, 2003; Hawthorne et al., 2004; Samuelowicz, 1987). Studies suggest the capacity of this approach to develop discipline-specific language-focused practices is questionable (for example, Liyanage & Birch, 2001). One study (Cruickshank et al., 2003) of a PTEP's responses to students at a leading Australian university outlines a remediation-based response integrated in the course of study. It involves study modules focussed on academic and workplace language, additional tutorial and mentoring support, and self-directed learning, but nonetheless aimed at effecting student adoption of the accepted local variety. A similar aim is implied in the recommendation of an Australian study targeting support of postgraduate Asian international pre-service teachers in the practicum component of a PTEP (Spooner-Lane et al., 2009) that a communication course be added to the program to develop cultural competence.

The other predominant response attributes difficulties experienced by students to differences in cultural practices, complicated by issues of language proficiency (Prescott & Hellstén, 2005). This response to difference recognizes what are perceived as culturally distinct practices and learning styles, and advocates concomitant adjustment by teaching staff to teach to difference and to support learners. At classroom and institutional levels, studies have aimed to identify or trial pedagogies that recognize and value difference (Carr, 2003; Hawthorne et al., 2004; Hudson & Morris, 2003; Prescott & Hellstén, 2005). There are numerous attempts to identify the characteristics of "internationalized" pedagogy, including a European model (Teekens, 2003), that aim to foster achievement of "internationalised learning outcomes" (Sanderson, 2011, p. 664). Sanderson (2011) proposes a model for internationalized pedagogy that:

> ... whilst being respectful of students as "cultural beings" (includes) ... assisting international students – many of whom speak English-as-an-Additional Language (EAL) – to make the transition to the local higher education setting ... (by) ... providing students with model answers to sample questions ... explaining discipline-specific vocabulary, eliciting

3

responses from students and providing them with clear, written instructions for oral presentations. (Sanderson, 2011, p. 665)

There are studies that report teachers' perceptions of the language capacities of students, but those which explore these capacities from a perspective other than standard Australian academic English are the exception. In fact, when it comes to pedagogic responses to internationalization of higher education the current literature is "relatively barren" (Sanderson, 2011, p. 661). In this chapter we use the perceptions of and responses of postgraduate teacher educators at an Australian university to the academic practices of Asian students to foreground the complexities of accommodating varied EAP practices within teacher education pedagogy.

CURRENT STUDY, FINDINGS AND DISCUSSION

The study was conducted at a metropolitan Australian university that offers long-established postgraduate teacher education programs in a variety of disciplines that attract significant numbers of international postgraduate students from Asia. We use interview data drawn from an ongoing research project involving purposively selected teacher educators who deliver a range of pre-service postgraduate courses preparing teachers to work in primary and secondary school sectors in a variety of classroom and specialist teacher roles. Semi-structured interviews were conducted to generate data that were transcribed for analysis. On the whole, postgraduate teacher educators' perceptions fell into two broad classes: (i) perceptions of English, its role in academia, and their own relation to this; and (ii) perceptions of academic language practices of students they teach. The predominant responses that flowed from these perceptions can, at best, be regarded as concessions rather than accommodations. In the next section, we discuss these using representative excerpts from the interview data.

Perceptions of English centre upon the notion of standards. The application of standards to student language practices in the classroom and academic assessment are seen to be a critical factor in establishing and maintaining institutional prestige and reputation, crucial to the employability of graduates and to the institution's capacity to attract future enrolments. In addition, the application of standards is seen as execution of a vicarious responsibility for the transmission and protection of language-related standards integral to the classroom practice of teacher graduates. Teacher educators position themselves as guardians and defenders of a pure or prestige variety of English at the core of standards in all three of these contexts.

Teacher educators have firm ideas about what constitutes acceptable and desirable student language use and they rely on the processes that filter student entry to PTEPs to ensure students are equipped with the requisite language skills and cultural resources necessary for successful participation. This reliance, however, is implicit in the data, evident more in perceptions of disabusal of the expectation. Perceptions of the language practices and performance of students who use different varieties of English that do not conform to teacher educators' expectations are reminiscent of native speakerist (Holliday, 2005) notions that the English language can and should be characterized as a standard, and superior, variety. What is missing from our data, by and large, is any perceptions of how academic discourses and practices that characterise students' socioeducational histories are embedded in their use of the English language (Anchimbie, 2009); whether students have prior academic experiences involving educated, local varieties of English, or they have learned English for the purposes of study, language use is "very much influenced by a particular culture of a writer's first language" (Phan, 2011, p. 24).

Uses of English in academic contexts in ways that do not conform to the practices and conventions valued by the interview participants are interpreted as errors and inappropriate, and become a target of remediation rather than an opportunity to exploit diverse cultural and linguistic resources. Teacher educators see remediation as an additional layer of responsibility, a burden, and some argue for tightening entry requirements thorough raising the minimum International English Language Testing Scores (IELTS) currently mandated because many students:

> ... find it very very difficult ... I think 6.5 (of IELTS) is wrong and I have some issues with the way the international office is accepting or using LOI (language of instruction) to allow students to come ... (P2: Lines 93-94)

Discrepancies between teacher educators' ideas of acceptable language use and student performance extend to the Englishes of some domestic students who are recent migrants:

> ... I have had a couple of people in my class who have got temporary residency so they are technically Australians but they come in as domestic students but they do have quite severe, in some cases, language difficulties and because they come in under temporary residency program as a domestic student ... (P4: Lines 141-144)

Responses of teacher educators to the perceptions of language use described can at best be regarded as concessions, rather than accommodative pedagogy. When referring to how varieties of English that do not accord with Western academic conventions in aspects such as choice of tenses, tenor, over-politeness, and generic structures can be accommodated, one teacher educator argued that:

> ... the big thing to me is whether or not meaning is affected, you know, if they can present their meaning, or they can construct an argument, a case, and that is understandable, then that's fine. I don't think they'll get extremely high marks, distinctions or high distinctions, because as I've said it's a Western university and they are coming to a Western university for a variety of reasons, but they want a qualification, a postgraduate qualification from a Western university, so I think we do them a disservice if what they get isn't that ... (P7: Lines 122-127)

This response is charged with additional implicit and explicit values attached to different varieties and academic practices. To begin, it is possible to overlook, to a limited extent, perceived shortcomings in student writing, but students whose work is characterised by some key features of other varieties cannot be considered for the best grades. Moreover, implicit in the suggestion that attribution of worth to another variety of English equates to "a disservice" to the student is a rejection and devaluation of other varieties of English and associated academic practices. In addition, the assumption that students who enrol in PTEPs in Australian universities want mastery of Australian academic English as part of their teaching qualification is an imposition on students whose objectives may be different. These values are imposed on students at every step in their experience; they must satisfy the requirement of language proficiency to gain entry and during their program of study they are penalised for using their own varieties of English that, in many cases, sufficed for the gaining of undergraduate degrees in their country of origin.

What is also being imposed on students is the perception that capacity to sustain institutional standing and reputation is an additional unspoken criterion applied in assessment of student academic output. For example, this is expressed in the following comment by a teacher educator:

> My feeling is that these students when they graduate from an Australian university, graduating with an Australian degree, and people will expect them to achieve the standard that is required by an Australian degree. When they go back to their home countries many of them go back to senior positions in the public service or in various education sectors and they get those positions based on the fact that they have an Australian postgraduate degree. I think it is doing a student disservice and doing a bit of damage to the university's reputation if the students aren't operating at that level ... (P1: Lines 89-95)

The suggestion that the quality of the degree and the work of the graduate will be judged by the use, or not, of Australian English, is based on assumptions about the values of those making the assessment, and in effect devalues more important elements of student learning. In the case of students who work in countries outside Australia, it devalues also any native varieties of English in use. This also suggests teacher educators perceive the capacity of students to use a particular variety of English as an integral graduate attribute that in turn operates as a vital indicator of the reputation of the institution. In such a view, any suggestion that what are perceived as universally accepted standards should accommodate other varieties of English and academic practices may be interpreted as threats to the standing of the institution that in turn jeopardize the reputations of all who are involved, both teacher educators themselves and graduates of the PTEPs.

Essentially, teacher educators in the study equate accommodation with the default response of remediation. Difference is noted, but not valued. Remediation accords a lesser value to the conventions currently used by the students and a variety of approaches to replacing these with more valued practices are evident in the responses of teacher educators in their efforts to provide language and learning support. Difference is equated with a need to adjust or adapt on the part of the student that can be achieved through remediation that, whether successful or not, is an appropriate mechanism for accommodation of students.

> So how do I accommodate it? I accommodate it by giving them a lot of one-on-one support and allowing them to resubmit assignments but I don't accommodate it by saying "Oh you're an international student and you don't have to reach the standard." ... I strongly encourage them to go to English Support but quite a few of them don't go to English Support. I reiterate that advice after their first assignment and some of them take it up ... (P1: Lines 131-135)

This is not accommodation of different varieties of English or EAP practices; this is rejection on the basis of a "standard." What is rejected, as the interview data revealed, extends far beyond the mechanics of language and accurate use. Many users of other varieties of English "have studied English grammar and vocabulary longer than they'd like to remember" (Fox, 1994, p. 115). What is captured by the umbrella notion of "standard" includes aspects of writing that are less clearly defined even in conventional Western academic terms by academics themselves (Dunworth & Kirkpatrick, 2003; Lea & Street, 1998). Notions such as relevance, clarity, argument development, voice, style, organization, analysis, and critical thinking, and concepts such as plagiarism, are bound up with cultural communication styles and not a lack of English proficiency (Fox, 1994; Phan, 2011). Applying the "standard" on these grounds rejects more than a variety of English or particular EAP practices; it rejects alternative ways of thinking and knowing while protecting the standard from hybridizing influences of the academic discourses of other Englishes.

Implications

Protection of a standard variety of English or Western EAP practices not only demonstrates a failure to grasp the dynamic nature of language, but also sits uneasily in an environment suffused by the rhetoric of internationalization. Advocates of internationalization, certainly at a policy level (Liddicoat, 2003), promote the benefits for local domestic Australian students of bringing the world and other ways of knowing to the Australian university classroom. This includes "reflecting on one's own culture, ways of constructing knowledge, understanding and being" (Sanderson, 2008, as cited in Mertova & Green, 2010, p. 4). Yet when Anglo-rhetorical academic conventions are imposed as the standard, that is, when the same standards are required of all students whatever their entry pathway and background, discourses and ways of constructing knowledge that are embedded in other varieties of English are devalued, marked as inferior to a variety that realizes Western paradigms of constructing knowledge. Almost two decades ago, reflecting on this situation in U.S. higher education, Fox (1994, p. 53) noted that:

> The dominant communication style and world view of the (Western) university, variously known as "academic writing," "analytical writing,"

> "critical thinking," or just plain "good writing," is based on assumptions and habits of mind that are derived from Western culture, and that this way of thinking and communicating is considered the most sophisticated, intelligent, and efficient by only a tiny fraction of the world's people. (Fox, 1994, p. xxi)

In this perspective, adoption of the default approach of remediation is a response that can be attributed to teacher educators' participation in a socio-educational context that, with respect to English, has traditionally promoted adherence to a single variety. The privileging of a variety, and investment with meanings about the capacities and performance of those who conform to the variety, has arguably generated "an idealised version of the 'Western student'" (Doherty & Singh, 2005, p. 53) that underpins problematization of international students (Kubota, 2001). An implicit assumption that BANA varieties of English and EAP practices are "somehow inherently superior in their knowledge of academic discourse and their ability to engage effectively in sophisticated language/literacy practices" (Duff, 2007, p. 01.06) has generated an idealized domestic student assumed to have the requisite literacy and capacities. This establishes the context for "otherization" that sanctions the application of a set of criteria for entry and subsequent performance for those who come from "outside." This is reflected in some subtle ways, even after graduation; for instance, in Australia existing provisions for teacher accreditation include application of language standards to teacher employment and registration, and thus exclusion of prospective candidates on the basis of language. In Queensland, all applicants must provide evidence of English language proficiency "except those who have completed the full four years of higher education study required for registration in English" (Queensland College of Teachers, 2011, p. 6). This exception is restricted to students from Australia, New Zealand, Canada, UK, USA, and the Republic of Ireland. Applicants meeting the requirements in all but this respect must provide evidence of English-language proficiency, for example:

> An IELTS (Academic) assessment with an average band score of 7.5 across all four skill areas of listening, speaking, reading and writing – with no score below 7 in any of the four skills areas and a score of no less than 8 in speaking and listening. (Queensland College of Teachers, 2011, p. 7)

This serves not only to discourage potential teachers who are not exempted from attempting to gain registration to teach but also effectively quarantines many students in schools from exposure to diverse varieties of English as legitimate and acceptable. In addition, in schools, diverse varieties of English are used by students who consequently have limited opportunities to encounter their variety as acceptable for educational discourse. In practical terms, this represents a dissonance between institutional demands for reproduction of a dominant discourse realized in "Anglo-rhetorical and disciplinary styles" (Kirkpatrick, 2009, p. 257) and daily dialogue in many Australian classrooms at all levels of education, including PTEP classrooms, in which, as sites of intercultural interaction, varieties of English are the means of communication.

Accommodating Asian varieties of English and academic practices in the pedagogy of PTEPs is fraught with difficulties in the current circumstances. Decades of educational policy and practice have fostered perceptions from an early stage that one variety must be the standard and that divergence is to be discouraged or penalized. Despite the multicultural nature of the wider Australian context, when it comes to education the medium of instruction and the standards that are applied to language use leave little room for diversity or the recognition and appreciation of hybridity that typifies Englishes and diverse academic practices in the world today. Many Australian teacher educators are themselves historical participants in this educational system as students and classroom teachers. Too few educators have had the opportunity to experience difference and what is different from their own experiences; what is needed are opportunities to perceive or recognize the dynamic nature of English and the implications for internationalized higher education of emergence of distinct varieties of English that function for expression of academic activity in other settings. It may be that a truly accommodative pedagogy demands a reassessment of what constitutes the English-language proficiency of teacher educators themselves to encompass what Canagarajah (1996, p. 233) terms a "multidialectal competence," in this instance not a production competence, but a "passive competence to understand new varieties."

The lack of understanding evident in the perceptions equally reflect a higher education sector that has embraced internationalization but that has not, despite a commitment to development of an accommodative pedagogy, succeeded in raising consciousness of educators about the language of instruction, English, in the globalised academic environment. Given the free movement of students in an internationalized education market in which BANA varieties of English and their academic practices dominate, the intermingling of these with other varieties and academic practices is an inevitable outcome and the continued application of one standard variety is under siege from emergence of a dynamic hybridity in academic English.

CONCLUSION

On the basis of ill-formed perceptions, current responses effectively devalue, demean, reject, and treat with condescension varieties of English and academic practices other than the standard. Lack of knowledge of the changing sociolinguistic landscape in the broader world limits responses to the reductive dichotomy of international or domestic student enrolment. If this is to change, pedagogy in PTEPs must become more open to hybridity that exploits other ways of using English and academic practices to engage in academic discourse. One approach to initiating change depends on providing teacher educators with a better understanding of the evolving linguistic landscape. The perceived ownership of English by the academy and its current monopoly of academic practices and discourses can be dislodged by continuing to develop a substantial body of theory and research, such as this volume presents and reports. Research that charts the linguistic landscape in academia, as in Phan's (2011) comparison of Vietnamese and Australian academic writing, is essential for understanding of Asian varieties of English and academic practices as valid, current, and tangible phenomena. This in turn must be complemented by research of pedagogic practices accommodative of alternative and accepted media of academic engagement. This can engender the possibility of a changed mindset, a benevolent but critical approach to understanding of the changing linguistic landscape, an attitudinal shift that will take time but one that needs to be nurtured in education from top to bottom.

REFERENCES

Altbach, P. G. (2004). Globalisation and the university: Myths and realities in an unequal world. *Tertiary Education and Management, 10*, 3-25.

Anchimbie, E. A. (2009). Local or international standards: Indigenized varieties of English at the crossroads. In F. Sharifian (Ed.), *English as an international language: Perspectives and pedagogical issues* (pp. 271-286). Bristol: Multilingual Matters.

Asmar, C. (2005). Internationalising students: Reassessing diasporic and local student difference. *Studies in Higher Education, 30*(3), 291-309.

Birch, G., & Liyanage, I. (2004). TESOL: Trojan horse of globalisation. In B. Bartlett, F. Bryer, & D. Roebuck (Eds.), *Educating: Weaving Research into Practice* (Vol. 1, pp. 93-102). Brisbane, Australia: Griffith University, School of Cognition, Language, and Special Education.

Borland, H., & Pearce, A. (2002). Identifying key dimensions of language and cultural disadvantage at university. *Australian Review of Applied Linguistics, 25*(2), 101-127.

Canagarajah, A. S. (1999). *Resisting linguistic imperialism in English teaching.* Oxford: Oxford University Press.

Carr, J. (2003). Culture through the looking glass: An intercultural experiment in sociolinguistics. In A. J. Liddicoat, S. Eisenchlas, & S. Trevaskes (Eds.), *Australian perspectives on internationalising education* (pp. 65-74). Melbourne: Language Australia.

Chanock, K., & Cargill, M. (2003). Who are Australian non-English-speaking-background (ANESB) students and how do they differ from other students? In A. Bartlett & K. Chanock (Eds.), *The missing part of the student profile jigsaw: Academic skills advising for Australian students from non-English speaking backgrounds* (pp. 11-21). Canberra: Academic Skills and Learning Centre, Australian National University.

Clerehan, R. (2004). *Wiser by degrees: Improving student learning about disciplinary discourse.* Paper presented at the "Transforming knowledge in to wisdom: Holistic approaches to teaching and learning," 2004 Annual International Conference of the Higher Education Research and Development Society of Australasia (HERDSA), 4-7 July, Miri, Sarawak. Retrieved 3/2/06 from http://www.herds2004.curtin.edu.au.my?Contributions/NRPapers?A030-jt.pdf.

Coley, M. (1999). The English language entry requirements of Australian universities for students of non-English speaking background. *Higher Education Research and Development, 18*(1), 7-17.

Cruickshank, K., Newell, S., & Cole, S. (2003). Meeting English language needs in teacher education: A flexible support model for non-English speaking background students. *Asia-Pacific Journal of Teacher Education, 31*(3), 239-247.

Department of Education Employment and Workplace Relations. (2011). Student 2010 full year: Selected higher education statistics. Retrieved 10/11/2011, from http://www.deewr.gov.au/HigherEducation/Publications/HEStatistics/Publications/Pages/2010StudentFullYear.aspx

Doherty, C., & Singh, P. (2005). How the West is done: Simulating Western pedagogy in a curriculum for Asian international students. In P. Ninnes & M. Hellsten (Eds.), *Internationalising higher education: Critical explorations of pedagogy and policy* (pp. 53-74). Dordrecht: Springer.

Duff, P. A. (2007). Problematising academic discourse socialisation. In H. Marriot, T. Moore, & R. Spence-Brown (Eds.), *Learning discourses and the discourse of learning* (pp. 1-18). Clayton, Victoria: Monash University ePress.

Dunworth, K., & Kirkpatrick, A. (2003). Redefining tertiary literacy – How literate do you need to be. In A. J. Liddicoat, S. Eisenchlas, & S. Trevaskes (Eds.), *Australian perspectives on internationalising education* (pp. 27-37). Melbourne: Language Australia.

Fox, H. (1994). *Listening to the world: Cultural issues in academic writing*. Urbana, IL: National Council of Teachers of English.

Gray, J. (2010). The branding of English and the culture of the new capitalism: Representations of the world of work in English language textbooks. *Applied Linguistics, 31*(5), 714-733.

Hawthorne, L., Minas, I. H., & Singh, B. (2004). A case study in the globalization of medical education: Assisting overseas-born students at the University of Melbourne. *Medical Teacher, 26*(2), 150-159.

Holliday, A. (2005). *The struggle to teach English as an international language*. Oxford: Oxford University Press.

Hudson, W., & Morris, S. (2003). University teaching and international education. In A. J. Liddicoat, S. Eisenchlas, & S. Trevaskes (Eds.), *Australian perspectives on internationalising education* (pp. 65-74). Melbourne: Language Australia.

Huxur, G., Mansfield, E., Nnazor, R., Schuetze, H., & Segawa, M. (1996). Learning needs and adaptation problems of foreign graduate student. *CSSHE Professional File, 15*, 1-16.

Jordan, R. R. (1997). *English for academic purposes: A guide and resource book for teachers*. Cambridge: Cambridge University Press.

Kirkpatrick, A. (2009). English as the international language of scholarship: Implications for dissemination of local knowledge. In F. Sharifian (Ed.), *English as an international language: Perspectives and pedagogical issues* (pp. 254-270). Bristol: Mulitlingual Matters.

Koehne, N. (2004). *Positioning international education and international students: Multiple discourses and discursive practices*. Paper presented at the AARE conference "Doing the Public Good: Positioning Education Research." Melbourne, Nov. 28-Dec. 2, 2004. Retrieved 19/8/05, from http://www.aare.edu.au/04pap/koe04870.pdf.

Kubota, R. (2001). Discursive construction of the images of U.S. classrooms. *TESOL Quarterly, 35*(1), 9-38.

Lea, M. R., & Street, B. V. (1998). Student writing in higher education: An academic literacies approach. *Studies in Higher Education, 23*(2), 157-172.

Liddicoat, A. J. (2003). Internationalisation as a concept in higher education: Perspectives from policy. In A. J. Liddicoat, S. Eisenchlas, & S. Trevaskes (Eds.), *Australian perspectives on internationalising education* (pp. 13-26). Melbourne: Language Australia.

Liyanage, I., & Birch, G. (2001). English for general academic purposes: Catering to discipline-specific needs. *Queensland Journal of Educational Research, 17*(1), 48-67.

Mertova, P., & Green, W. (2010). *Internationalising teaching and learning: Perspectives and issues voiced by senior academics at one Australian university*. Paper presented at the 21st ISANA International Education Association Conference, The Crown Promenade, Melbourne, VIC, http://www.proceedings.com.au/isana/docs/2010/paper_mertova.pdf

Phan, L.-H. (2007). Towards a critical notion of appropriation of English as an international language. *Journal of English as an International Language, 1*(1), 48-60.

Phan, L.-H. (2011). The writing and culture nexus: Writers' comparisons of Vietnamese and English academic writing. In L.-H. Phan & B. Baurain (Eds.), *Voices, identities, negotiations, and conflicts: Writing academic English across cultures* (pp. 23-40). Bingley, U.K.: Emerald.

Prescott, A., & Hellstén, M. (2005). Hanging together even with non-native speakers: The international student transition experience. In P. Ninnes & M. Hellstén (Eds.), *Internationalizing higher education: Critical explorations of pedagogy and policy* (pp. 75-95). Dordrecht: Springer.

Queensland College of Teachers. (2011). *Application guidelines: Teacher registration*. Brisbane: Queensland College of Teachers. Retrieved from http://www.qct.edu.au/PDF/PSU/Teacher_Registration_Guidelines.pdf.

Ruby, A. (2008). Reshaping the university in an era of globalization. In J. Z. Spade & J. H. Ballantine (Eds.), *Schools and society: A sociological approach to education* (pp. 436-456). Thousand Oaks, CA: Pine Forge Press.

Samuelowicz, K. (1987). Learning problems of overseas students: Two sides of a story. *Higher Education Research and Development, 6*(2), 121-133.

Sanderson, G. (2011). Internationalisation and teaching in higher education. *Higher Education Research & Development, 30*(5), 661-676.

Spooner-Lane, R., Tangen, D., & Campbell, M. (2009). The complexities of supporting Asian international pre-service teachers as they undertake practicum. *Asia-Pacific Journal of Teacher Education, 37*(1), 79-94.

Teekens, H. (2003). The requirement to develop specific skills for teaching in an intercultural setting. *Journal of Studies in International Education, 7*(1), 108-119.

Walker, A. W. (2010). *Language diversity and classroom dialogue: Negotiation of meaning by students in an internationalised postgraduate classroom.* Unpublished doctoral dissertation, Griffith University, Brisbane, Australia.

Wilson, K. (2003). Assisting ANESB students to acquire academic language skills. In A. Bartlett & K. Chanock (Eds.), *The missing part of the student profile jigsaw: Academic skills advising for Australian students from non-English speaking backgrounds.* Canberra: Academic Skills and Learning Centre, A.N.U.

Indika Liyanage
Griffith Institute for Educational Research
Griffith University
Australia

Tony Walker
Griffith Institute for Educational Research
Griffith University
Australia

YANMEI GAO & BRENDAN BARTLETT

2. OPPORTUNITIES AND CHALLENGES FOR NEGOTIATING APPROPRIATE EAP PRACTICES IN CHINA

INTRODUCTION

English for Academic Purposes (EAP) emerged in the early 1980s, "as a relatively fringe branch of English for Specific Purposes (ESP)" (Hyland, 2006, p. 1) to meet the needs of internationalization of higher education, and has now grown into a major force in English-language teaching and research around the world (Hyland, 2006). Its concentration, according to Jordan (1997, p. 1), is on "those communicative skills in English which are required for study purposes in formal educational systems." Hyland and Hamp-Lyons (2002, p. 2) noted that EAP "... focuses on the specific communicative needs and practices of particular groups in academic contexts. It means grounding instruction in an understanding of the cognitive, social and linguistic demands of specific academic disciplines." This targets the aim of teaching English not only to improve English-language proficiency, but also to equip students with communicative skills appropriate for engaging in various academic activities, such as being learning-active in lectures and seminars, participating effectively as learners in discussions, and giving oral presentations. Interest in EAP, and systematic involvement with EAP practices, has stretched far beyond Anglophone countries. Unsurprisingly, these practices have also found their way into the educational systems of countries and districts that have come to use English as a medium of instruction (MOI) in higher education, such as Hong Kong (Evans, 2003), Indonesia (Sultan, Borland, & Eckersley, 2012), Malaysia (Hudson, 2009), Pakistan (Ashraf & Hakim, this volume), and China (Yu & Yuan, 2005).

The internationalization of higher education has great impact on its curricula and MOI. One consequence is the rapid increase in the number of courses and degrees taught through the medium of English in universities worldwide (Gill & Kirkpatrick, 2013). In 2001, the Ministry of Education in China began an extensive promotion of bilingual teaching using English as the MOI. It continues to encourage its universities to cultivate academic courses, especially professional subjects such as information technology, biotechnology, new-material technology, finance, and foreign trade, that use English or other foreign languages as the MOI, believing this is the best means to enhance international competitiveness and to prepare students for international cooperation and exchange (Gill & Kirkpatrick, 2013; Sun & Xu, 2012). This new orientation has posed mounting pressure to both

I. Liyanage & T. Walker (eds.), English for Academic Purposes (EAP) in Asia, 13–31.
© 2014 Sense Publishers. All rights reserved.

the academic departments and the College English programs in most universities. Allied to this have been significant issues confronting both students and their instructors. To prepare students for the academic courses that use English as the MOI in junior or senior years, specific EAP courses now have been introduced into a small number of universities in China. Meanwhile the majority of universities has not yet resolved how best to cope with the new pressures of extending current arrangements to include such new measures.

As a sub-branch of English-language teaching, EAP is different from teaching English for General Purposes (EGP – known as College English at the tertiary level). In the Chinese higher educational context, EAP is a transition from College English to programs of study delivered in English as the MOI. The two share the same target group of learners, but with different teaching purposes, foci, and approaches. On the one hand, EAP practices address a rounded set of academic language skills for academic studies, and great importance is attached to needs analysis as a systematic way to identify the specific sets of skills, texts, linguistic forms and communicative practices that a particular group of learners must acquire (Hyland & Hamp-Lyons, 2002) for the specific nature and circumstances of their work. On the other hand, and in contrast, College English courses provide instruction sharply focussed on grammar, vocabulary, and other general language skills, and are more general in orientation, placing no special emphasis on identifying and meeting specific needs of specific groups of learners.

In the past few years, researchers and administrators have been advocating a new wave of reform in English teaching and learning in China, aiming to promote English for Specific Purposes (ESP) or EAP at tertiary level as a substitute for the current College English programs (Cai & Liao, 2010a; Qin, 2003; Yang, 2010). Yet, this initiative has not been fully understood and enacted by the majority of College English instructors and the administrations that support them. Additionally, whether college students need ESP or EAP courses to prepare them for future programs of study in which the MOI is English is an unresolved question for some. In this chapter we report a case study carried out at Peking University to explore the opportunities and challenges inherent in contemplations of appropriate EAP in China.

The Local Context of English Education at Tertiary Level in China

The past three decades have witnessed two major waves of reform in English education at the tertiary level in Mainland China (Wen & Hu, 2007). The first, from the 1980s to 1990s, was marked by the division of its College English teaching syllabus into one College English Teaching (CET) Syllabus for Arts students and another for Science and Technology students. During this period, two sets of College English textbooks were compiled and students from Arts and Science academic backgrounds used the corresponding English textbooks while attending their courses. The emphasis of this period was on macro-skills of reading and writing.

The second wave was marked by introduction of the College English Curriculum Requirements (Department of Higher Education of Ministry of Education of the People's Republic of China, 2004). Under these new requirements, emphasis on reading and writing shifted to include listening and speaking. To cope with sharp increases in college enrolment, computer-mediated facilities and new teaching models were introduced and online autonomous learning became an integral part of College English programs. Concurrently, from 2001, school children in urban areas began their studies of English from Grade 3 (Ministry of Education of the People's Republic of China, 2001). As this meant English education commenced much earlier than previously, it is unsurprising that English-language proficiencies of recent college student cohorts have improved. An increasing number of universities responded by starting to cultivate advanced courses beyond the basic skills training courses that had been used previously. This has pushed College English teachers to re-evaluate the levels of difficulty of both textbooks and study programs.

Thus, there has been a growing interest in EAP among EFL instructors and researchers. This is reflected in the sharp increase of periodical publications of research papers. According to Jiang and Li (2010), from 1985 to 2008, only about 110 articles on ESP were published in the top 10 Chinese Social Sciences Citation Index (CSSCI) journals of foreign-language teaching and research. These research articles fall mainly into two categories: those providing general introductions of western EAP practices (Ju, 2006; Yao, 2001), such as EAP practices in the UK (Zhang, 2004), and those concerning exploration of the feasibilities of introduction the EAP practices in typical models used by particular Western universities, such as the EAP model of Wollongong in Australia (Zhang, 2006), and the Romanian model of EAP seminars (Zhu, 2006). More recently, the emphasis has shifted, with a great many papers devoted to exploring the possibilities and feasibilities of EAP practices in Chinese EFL contexts. Cai (2010, 2011a, 2011b, 2012a) and Cai and Liao (2010a, 2010b) have carried out a series of investigations exploring the feasibilities of implementing EAP in China and the relationship between current College English courses and ESP/EAP courses. They come to the conclusion that it is time to cultivate EAP courses in Chinese universities. W. M. Zhang, Zhang, and Liu (2011) introduce the Tsinghua model of EAP. It is implied, though not explicitly inscribed, that the current program of College English in the Chinese English educational system has fulfilled its historical goals and is ready to be replaced by EAP in the interests of progressing quality (Cai, 2012a; Cai & Liao, 2010a).

The underlying question is whether EAP is more appropriate as complement to, or as substitute for, the current College English programs; debates and discussions on this question began nearly a decade ago (Cai, 2012a, 2012b; Qin, 2003; Yang, 2010). Assessments of the current provision, and needs analyses for EAP carried out by a number of universities in attempts to resolve the issue (Cai, 2012b; Xia, 2003), show that more than half the participants felt dissatisfied with the current College English programs (Cai, 2010; Xia, 2003) and recorded strong demands for EAP, not only to prepare students and staff for programs that use English as the

MOI, but also to assist with study abroad and engagement with lectures given by specialists who are native speakers of English (NSE) (Cai, 2012a).

To meet these demands, EAP courses have been introduced at several universities in China. These courses follow two different patterns: typical Western EAP practices and hybrid EAP practices which combine elements of Western EAP practices and elements of local EFL practices. Typical Western EAP practices are applied mainly in universities where joint programs are carried out, the most influential being The University of Nottingham Ningbo, China (UNNC) and Xi'an Jiaotong Liverpool University. In the former, typical British EAP courses are provided by the Centre of English Language Education. Here, it is strictly the Nottingham model of EAP that is implemented and instructors in this program are native speakers of English selected and trained by The University of Nottingham, UK. In Xi'an Jiaotong Liverpool University, specially designed EAP modules are offered to both undergraduates and postgraduates.

Various hybrid models are implemented mainly in state-owned universities, for instance, Fudan University, where EAP courses were designed on the basis of ESP, with stronger orientations towards the target academic disciplines, such as Academic English for Humanities, for Social Sciences, for Business, for Medicine, and for Science and Engineering (Cai, 2012a). In the instance of Tsinghua University, EAP courses follow a different pattern wherein there is a combination of language skills training with general academic targets provided. Its EAP courses are further divided into eight subdivisions, including EAP Reading and Writing (Bands 1-4), and EAP Listening and Speaking (Bands 1-4) (Zhang et al., 2011).

BACKGROUND OF THE STUDY

While the pioneers have been exploring the feasibilities of hybrid models, such as those adopted in Fudan and Tsinghua Universities, the great majority of universities in China has not yet joined them. Peking University is one of these. With its well-established tradition of foreign-language education and an emphasis on developing "students' ability to use English in an all-round way" (Department of Higher Education of Ministry of Education of the People's Republic of China, 2004, p. 24), College English programs at Peking University have cultivated a double systems model in the past two decades to meet the varied needs of its EFL learners. One of them is the system of basic College English courses, ranging from CET Bands 1 to 4, in which students of each new cohort are placed into bands according to their results on placement tests. The second system is the advanced College English courses, provided by EFL instructors, including Advanced Reading and Writing, Advanced Academic Listening, English Classics, American and British Cultures, etcetera. Students who have accomplished College English Band 4 studies go directly into the second system.

Apart from College English programs, some academic Departments and Colleges offer EAP courses, and academic courses delivered in English MOI are also offered to undergraduates. Our survey revealed that 85 students who were taking College English courses when the survey was conducted had already completed some English MOI academic courses in their own Colleges. The divisions of the English-related programs for undergraduates at Peking University are summarized in Table 1.

Table 1. English-related programs at Peking University

Course Providers	College English Section		Academic Departments & Colleges	
Courses	College English comprehensive courses	College English advanced courses	EAP	Academic courses using English as MOI
Target Undergraduate students	Freshmen to sophomore	Freshmen to senior	Sophomore to senior	Sophomore to senior
Instructors	College English instructors	College English instructors	EAP instructors	Academic instructors
Course content	Basic language skills	Advanced skills training, culture, etc.	EAP (e.g., Legal English)	Academic content (e.g., Cognitive Psychology)

In the last 10 years, English MOI academic courses like those provided at Peking University have been offered in many other universities all over China. Thus, Peking University is not a special case in its adoption of the double systems model. Under such circumstances, the future of EAP programs as bridges between the present College English programs and academic courses in English medium offered by individual academic departments and colleges remains a question to be explored. If there is will for EAP programs to be developed, then it is unclear what challenges instructors and administrators will face in implementing it into their English education system. Accordingly, we sought to inform some resolution of the issue with the following research questions:
– Is it necessary for the current College English programs to be extended to EAP courses for all students?
– If EAP practices are to be implemented, what will be the major challenges?

INSTRUMENTS AND METHOD

Survey

The study reported in this chapter involved both staff and students at Peking University. To investigate the first question, a survey was used to explore College English students' perceptions of academic English-language skills they saw as essential for their academic study, and to capture their views of the necessity of

17

EAP instruction. The survey was designed on the basis of a needs analysis (Cai, 2012a), with attention to micro-skills of academic listening and reading (Jordan, 1997) and academic writing skills (Etherington, 2005). It focussed on students' assessments of difficulties of the academic tasks, self-assessment of academic English-language skills, and evaluation of the importance of EAP instruction. The survey consisted of 45 items grouped into four parts.

In Part I, there were three open questions concerning students' grades, academic backgrounds, and experiences of EAP or academic courses using English as the MOI. Part II contained one multiple-choice question on students' needs for academic English skills and eight questions on their assessment of the levels of difficulty of EAP tasks. The five choices provided for best outcome in relation to students' needs were (a) to enrol in academic courses or bilingual academic courses, (b) to use academic reading, (c) to attend lectures given by English-speaking specialists, (d) to study abroad in the future, and (e) no need at all. To answer this question, participants were not limited to one selection. Responses to the eight questions on difficulties of academic tasks were ranked along a five-point Likert scale (1=very easy, 5=very difficult). Part III contained 28 items on students' perceptions of academic English-language skills essential for academic study. These covered four main areas of language skills: listening (6 items), reading (9 items), speaking (2 items, based on Jordan, 1997) and writing (11 items, based on Etherington, 2005). Responses to items in this part were also ranked along a five-point Likert scale (1=low/limited, 5=high). Part IV (1 item) focussed on students' evaluations of the importance of EAP instruction. Choices again were ranked along a five-point Likert scale (1=not at all important, 5=extremely important). Items in Part I, II, and IV were given in Chinese and those in Part III were in English.

Students surveyed were all undergraduates enrolled in advanced courses provided by the university's College English section in the semester the study was undertaken, that is, they had accomplished the basic comprehensive courses of College English. The surveys were distributed by College English instructors in their classes and were completed during a break. Two hundred and forty-three students were asked to fill out the surveys. Incomplete surveys were discarded. The final tally was 216 completed surveys.

Focus Group Interview

Data for the second question were generated using focus group interviews with College English students and instructors to probe their various perceptions of the current provision and consideration of implementing EAP at this university. Thirteen students were purposively selected to represent a range of academic specialties, including Mathematical Sciences, Physics, Life Sciences, Chemistry, Urban and Environmental Sciences, Law, Government, and Archaeology and Museology. All the students interviewed were taking advanced courses in the semester when the study was undertaken. The instructors were 10 College English staff who were teaching advanced courses in the semester the study was conducted. Their ages ranged from 30 to 55 years and their teaching experience from 7 to 30 years. All held an MA credential specializing in English literature or linguistics.

Interview questions for the students were designed to explore the following themes: experiences of studying academic courses delivered in English as the MOI or English and Chinese bilingually; difficulties in fulfilling academic tasks in the medium of English, such as following lectures or writing academic essays; understanding of the relationship between College English and EAP; and views of EAP practices in the future. Questions put to instructors during the interview focussed on their perceptions of the relationship between College English and EAP and the necessity of implementing EAP at this university. Chinese language was used in the interviews, and recordings were transcribed; data included in this chapter were translated into English.

ANALYSIS AND FINDINGS

Survey Data

Four sets of descriptive statistics that include overall frequencies, percentages, means, and standard deviations were collected from the survey using the Statistical Package for the Social Sciences (SPSS) software. The first set concerned the students' needs, the second concentrated on their assessments of difficulty of academic tasks, the third were their perceptions of their academic language skills, and the last were their evaluations of the importance of EAP instruction.

Data showed that 52.8% of students had opportunity to enrol in academic courses delivered in the medium of English, 87% of them had academic reading tasks involving English, 74.5% could attend lectures given by English-speaking specialists, and 66.7% planned to study abroad in the future. Only five students indicated they had no need at all. This absence of need for English seems related to their specialties – two of them were majoring in Japanese, two in Chinese, and one in Archaeology, none of which had particular functional connection to English.

Data from the students' assessment of the levels of difficulty of the academic tasks are listed in Table 2. Among the eight academic tasks, the three most difficult were *academic writing, oral presentation,* and *guessing the meaning of unknown words. Academic reading* was moderately difficult. The one with which they felt most at ease was *note-taking.*

The mean scores of students' responses to perceptions of their academic-language skills (four macro-skills and 28 micro-skills) are listed in Tables 3 and 4.

Table 2. Students' assessment of the levels of difficulty of academic tasks

Academic tasks	Mean	S.D.
Lecture	3.13	0.98
Note-taking	2.81	0.96
Understanding main idea	3.15	1.01
Oral presentation	3.54	1.00
Seminars	3.10	0.92
Guess the meaning of unknown words	3.31	1.05
Academic reading	3.23	1.04
Academic writing (reports or theses)	3.54	1.02

Table 3. Students' self-assessment of the four macro-skills

Macro-skills	Mean	S.D.
Reading	3.29	0.82
Listening	3.26	0.85
Writing	3.13	0.88
Speaking	2.89	0.92

Among the four macro-skills, students ranked their reading as most skilful, followed by listening and writing, with speaking as most limited. All standard deviations were below 1.0, indicating tight clustering among the choices made by respondents in each of the macro-skill ratings.

Within each group, among different items, mean scores for students' perceptions of their individual micro-skills varied slightly (Table 4). Among the six micro-skills of listening, the highest was *ability to identify topic of lecture and follow topic development*, followed by the *ability to identify purpose and scope of lecture* and *ability to recognize key lexical items related to subject/topic*. The most limited was *ability to follow lecture despite differences in accent and speed*.

Among the nine micro-skills of reading, means ranged from 3.09 to 3.43 (see Table 4). The skill, *distinguishing between important and less important items* had the highest mean (3.43). It was followed by *drawing inferences and conclusions* and *distinguishing between relevant and irrelevant information. Deducing unknown words* had the lowest mean (3.09).

There were two micro-skills of speaking: *pronunciation and intonation*, and *oral presentation*. Students gave the first a higher value (3.03) in comparison with the second (2.75). Both values are much lower than those for all other micro-skills, indicating that students perceived their speaking skills to be the most limited.

Following Etherington (2005), we investigated 11 academic writing skills, including *clarity of argument and writing, grammatical accuracy, vocabulary variety*, and *avoidance of plagiarism*. Means of the 11 micro-skills vary from 2.82 to 3.38. The highest was for *avoidance of plagiarism*. Comparatively strong skills

Table 4. Students' perceptions of their academic micro-skills

Macroskill	Micro-skills	Mean S.D.
Listening	Ability to identify purpose and scope of lecture	3.34 0.85
	Ability to identify topic of lecture and follow topic development	3.44 0.82
	Ability to identify relationships among units within discourse	3.27 0.78
	Ability to infer relationships (e.g., cause, effect, conclusion)	3.26 0.81
	Ability to recognize key lexical items related to subject/topic	3.31 0.8
	Ability to follow lecture despite differences in accent and speed	2.92 0.93
Reading	Prediction	3.29 0.75
	Skimming (reading quickly for the main idea or gist)	3.27 0.87
	Scanning (reading quickly for a specific piece of information)	3.24 0.87
	Distinguishing between factual and non-factual information	3.27 0.8
	Distinguishing between important and less important items	3.43 0.83
	Distinguishing between relevant and irrelevant information	3.33 0.81
	Drawing inferences and conclusions	3.4 0.8
	Deducing unknown words	3.09 0.82
	Understanding text organization	3.29 0.77
Speaking	Pronunciation and intonation	3.03 0.91
	Oral presentation	2.75 0.92
Writing	Clarity of argument and writing	3.26 0.75
	Logical development of argument	3.32 0.83
	Grammatical accuracy	3.23 0.84
	Grammatical variety	3.0 0.87
	Vocabulary accuracy	3.09 0.86
	Vocabulary variety	2.82 0.88
	Use of suitable style	3.06 0.83
	Use of graphics/illustrations	3.11 0.81
	Use of references/use of quotations	3.03 0.89
	Standard of word processing	3.08 0.81
	Avoidance of plagiarism	3.38 1.09

included, *logical development of argument* and *clarity of argument and writing*. *Vocabulary variety* was seen as comparatively weak. The skills of *grammatical variety* and *use of references/use of quotations* were also ranked at lower levels.

Data show also students' evaluation of the importance of EAP instruction. Generally, these are very positive; 85.2% thought EAP instruction to be important or very important.

Interview Data

Data collected from the focus group interviews provided more diverse and thought-provoking information about students' and instructors' perceptions of the current courses at this university and about their views of implementing EAP. Data from interviews of students were summarized around two features: expressions of needs for training, and evaluations of the current EAP courses and academic courses using English as the MOI. The categorical collation of students' statements of experiences is shown in Table 5. While there was overlap in their attendances at different courses, 8 of the 13 had participated in EAP courses or academic courses delivered in English as the MOI which had been given by instructors from their own academic departments. One had a typical Western EAP course; one had a local model of EAP; two had academic courses delivered by NSE instructors. Six of them had experience of bilingual academic courses.

Table 5. Students' experiences of EAP and academic courses using English as MOI

Attendance	EAP Courses		Academic courses using English as MOI	
	NSE instructor	*Bilingual Chinese instructor*	*NSE instructor*	*Bilingual Chinese instructor*
N. of courses taken	1	1	4	11
N. of attendees	1	1	3	6

In relation to needs for EAP training, students had found it very hard to fully adapt to the academic requirements of the academic courses using English as the MOI, despite the existing support structures. This was especially the case in courses given by NSE instructors. This corroborates our findings from the survey. The following excerpts (students, S1-13 and instructors, I1-10) illustrate this trend:

S1: We only have one academic course given by a native English speaker. ... The most difficult task with this course is writing, the research essay. There are mainly two problems: technical terms and writing strategy. As we have no training in writing academic essays in English, this is absolutely a big problem.

S2: All our courses (Mathematics) were given in Chinese. Even in Chinese, they are still difficult. But I went to the University of California at Berkeley to attend the summer session last year. The most difficult tasks for me then were listening and vocabulary.

S3: Academic writing is still the major problem. You may have some ideas, but you don't know how to put them into English. We need a lot of training in rhetoric and academic writing skills.

S5: Many students found the courses given by foreign instructors very difficult. This does not mean that the content is difficult. The hardest part is the English environment, lectures, seminars, reading, essay-writings and examinations, all in English.... At the beginning of the course, our instructor told us that he had been invited here to teach history, not English. Therefore, he would not slow down to wait for those whose English was poor ....

The deficiency in training for academic writing was felt deeply by almost all interviewees who had experienced the need to write academic essays in English. The English-only environments of the classrooms of NSE instructors also had placed considerable pressure on students.

Concerning the second feature, students' evaluations of the current EAP courses and academic courses using English as the MOI were positive. The typical Western EAP course and the academic courses given by NSE instructors, though difficult, were very well-received by those students who took them. Students 3 and 5 articulated the profound effect of these courses:

S3: We had a typical EAP course (as you have described) given by a professor who was a native speaker of English – the Scientific Research Skills – basic skills for Biology. The instructor taught us the academic conventions of biology, including academic writing and oral presentation. This helped greatly in my reading and vocabulary .... As for the gains from this kind of course, accumulation of vocabulary is one. What's more important is the adaptation to English expressions .... EAP and academic courses delivered in the medium of English deepened my understanding of the importance of English. I realized then that English was opening a window for me, enabling me to get access to knowledge that I had not touched before.

S5: We had two courses given by two native speakers of English. Every week we had to read quantities of materials – books, speeches, archives, etc. all in English. We had a lot of troubles with them .... But we learned a great deal, especially in vocabulary .... Most important, I learned the American academic writing conventions. Whether you do research or not, these are very valuable practical strategies.

The students concerned had formed a clear view of what they have gained from these courses and believed that they had gained much more than peers who had not had such experiences. Compared with the typical Western EAP and academic courses given by NSE instructors, bilingual academic courses are not considered to be difficult. Students' perceptions of what had been gained from bilingual courses included the accumulation of technical vocabulary and the improvement of reading comprehension:

S7: Bilingual courses familiarized me with subject vocabulary, writing styles typical for my academic field and research methods.

S11: Bilingual courses mainly introduce knowledge or help improve academic skills.

S8: The two bilingual academic courses helped enlarge my vocabulary and improve my academic reading skills. I still have a lot of difficulty in academic writing, as we did not have such kind of training.

Bilingual instructors usually prepared their PowerPoint slides in English. This familiarized students with the concepts and theories in their own fields and increased exposure to the contextualized vocabulary. Although the motif of cultivating EAP, bilingual, and MOI academic courses is the same – to prepare students for international cooperation and exchange (Sun & Xu, 2012) – the effects are very different. From the comments of S3 and S5, we see that the typical Western EAP course and the MOI courses delivered by NSE instructors are much more successful in this respect. Students gained enormously from their greater exposure to the academic conventions, writing strategies, vocabulary, etcetera. Judged from the ultimate goal of leading students into the international academic arena, bilingual courses are quite limited.

Data from the instructor group tell us much about how instructors perceive the relationship between College English and EAP. First, with rich experiences in teaching advanced courses to post-CET Band 4 students, most of the instructors were confident about the positive effects of College English instruction on students' academic language skills. Although advanced courses are not tailored finely for students from diverse academic backgrounds, in the opinion of Instructor 1 there are plenty of alternatives and students do have the option to find courses that fit well with their own learning needs concerning English macro-skills:

I1: I think our advanced courses give students a lot of opportunities to follow their own hearts. Say, if a student is weak at writing, s/he may choose to study writing for a semester. If s/he finds s/he is limited in vocabulary, s/he may take the course of English Lexicology. I think this reflects the nature of autonomous learning.

A second trend in these qualitative data is that most instructors have an understanding of EAP and know about the differences and similarities between College English advanced courses and EAP courses. Some of them thought that they had already embedded some elements of EAP in their own advanced courses. According to Alexander, Argent, and Spencer's (2008) distinctions, a large number of College English advanced courses at this university are similar to EAP in language content, language-skills balance, materials, text choice, and text exploitation. Instructors feel strongly about these similarities, as evident in the following comment from Instructor 10:

I10: Although we do not call our courses EAP courses, we have most of the EAP elements in them. In our advanced writing courses, we teach students how to develop arguments, how to organize their ideas step by step. The topics may be humanistic ones, but the strategies are universal among all academic disciplines. With these basic writing skills, students will be able to fulfil academic writing tasks in their own fields. That's why we do not think it is necessary to develop specific English courses to meet the specific needs of learners from different academic departments.

Some of the advanced courses within the general framework of College English programs were inspired by the typical EAP models in academic departments. Therefore, some advanced courses given by College English instructors, for example, Listening Skills in Academic English, and those given by academic instructors share many similarities. Feelings about this closeness were expressed also by students who had taken EAP courses given by Chinese instructors from their own departments, for example, in the opinion of Student 13, the EAP course provided in her own department should better be categorized into College English advanced courses.

Both the students and the instructors were asked about their views of the implementation of EAP at this university. Students were concerned about the orientation of courses. Perceptions of disproportionate representation of culture and literature content in both College English basic courses and advanced courses were evident in accounts from almost all students interviewed. Those in Science, such as Student 4, expressed their dissatisfaction with this imbalance explicitly:

S4: Personally speaking, the current College English courses, especially the textbooks, have put too much emphasis on humanities and literature. I hope we could have more courses which can help me improve my academic English-language skills, especially reading and writing. I feel this is also what most science students expect from an English course in academic settings.

Students' expectations of science-oriented English courses or academic courses delivered in English as the MOI echoed Cai and Liao's (2010a) claims that the orientation of future college English should be ESP or EAP, and not English for humanities.

Instructors were asked about their perceptions of the necessity of implementing EAP in the current provision and how this might be done. Among the 10 instructors interviewed, 3 thought it unnecessary and 1 felt uncertain, but 6 agreed on the necessity of implementing EAP:

I1: We should have developed such courses years ago.

I3: I think it is very necessary to cultivate EAP courses.

I8: We should provide both sound College English courses and corresponding academic English courses.

As to who is more appropriate to teach EAP courses, instructors differed. Three thought that both College English and bilingual academic instructors were suitable, while another three thought academic instructors only should teach such courses.

Four suggested that EAP requires joint endeavours from both College English instructors and instructors from the academic departments:

I1: Both of us (College English instructors and academic instructors) could do it, though emphases will be put on different aspects.

I3: Even though this may put my job at a risk, I would say that EAP courses should be given by two kinds of instructors: either academic instructors with high English-language proficiencies or College English instructors who have a passable knowledge of the subject matter areas.

I5: (If EAP is to be implemented,) it would be better if College English instructors can join hands with instructors from the academic departments. These instructors can teach subject knowledge (e.g., vocabulary) and College English instructors the general academic language skills.

Though implicitly conveyed, all of the instructors had some sense of a deep impact on them personally should EAP be implemented in their programs or at the university.

DISCUSSION

Within the limitations of the size and scope of this study, findings suggest that there is great opportunity for implementing EAP practices at this university to complement current provision of support for students, but that real challenges need to be recognized and addressed if this is to be successful.

Data from both the survey and interviews demonstrate that the two groups of stakeholders recognized the importance of EAP instruction in the current academic settings of this university. Students felt an urgent need to improve their academic language skills to cope better with the requirements of course studies and to prepare more fully for future pursuits. This is not surprising as data from our needs analysis, which are in the range reported elsewhere (see Cai, 2010), revealed that 56.5% of students in our sample take academic courses given in English as the MOI, and 58.1% plan to study abroad in the future. As more and more programs using English as the MOI are offered in Chinese universities, it is not hard to imagine the demand will increase for systematic attention to improvement of support for students in acquiring academic English-language skills and for those who will assist them in doing so.

Backing for implementing EAP outright, rather than enhancing current College English advanced courses with an infusion of EAP-like features, comes from the students' optimistic assessment of EAP and academic courses given in English as the MOI. The great gains of the two students who had completed these courses suggest the potential for success of such practices at this university. However, among the eight departments in question, only two could afford such practices. Therefore, more funding is needed and/or more practical and less-costly models need to be developed if EAP courses are to be implemented in their own right to meet the needs of the majority of students. The models of Tsinghua University and Fudan University (Cai, 2012a; Zhang et al., 2011) present one avenue for exploration in this respect.

Challenges emerge from both the students' self-assessments of their academic language skills essential for academic studies and the instructors' perceptions of responsibility for creating and teaching EAP courses. Students' self-assessments indicated a gap between perceptions of what they can do and what they are expected to do. On the one hand, consistency between their perceptions of the levels of difficulty of the academic tasks and self-assessment of their corresponding academic language capacities justifies their evaluation of the importance of EAP instruction. On the other, which model is more appropriate to bridge this gap, and how the bridging will be done, are questions to be thoroughly considered and explored in any specific setting before an EAP model is to be implemented.

A second challenge for implementing EAP at this university results from the divergence in instructors' opinions about who would shoulder the responsibility for designing and teaching EAP courses. Four instructors from the focus group interviews advocated the implementation of EAP practices through joint efforts from both College English instructors and instructors delivering courses in the academic departments and colleges. Instructors of EAP and of academic courses in the academic departments and colleges usually have a BA or MA in English language and literature, and the bilingual academic instructors have studied abroad in an English-speaking university, or visited one. Collaboration would address Instructor 3's view that a passable knowledge of subject matter areas is essential for those who are to teach EAP. Considered with students' positive comments about bilingual instructors' effectiveness, these findings have implications for what needs to be done to ensure quality EAP is delivered. Certainly, College English instructors at most universities in China have their academic origins in one major source – they are graduates from English language and literature programs of higher education. It is possible this homogeneity in educational background has restricted the scope of courses that instructors have offered and feasible that steps beyond designing coursework within the field of language, linguistics, and literature are challenging for them – and would be for future EAP instructors with similar backgrounds. This is not so much regarding their capacities as educators, but rather in relation to their confidence in specific content disciplines where they are novices rather than experts. Professional development will be needed to help the available and new instructional workforce to develop and establish productive balance between instructors' dual roles as learners and teachers. It is a situation tailor-made for action learning (Bartlett & Piggot-Irvine, 2008) – a low-cost, high-yield approach to improving support for instructors while enhancing, rather than risking, their career development.

CONCLUSION

EAP is a new English education model in the Chinese EFL context. This contrasts somewhat with its longer and evidence-supported existence as a successful approach in both English-speaking countries and several non-English-speaking countries. Newness in China is itself contextualized by the profile of take-up across Chinese universities. In the past few years, localized EAP patterns have been employed in some universities while the majority has taken a more conservative wait-and-see position – an onlooker's commitment to what may or may not be better than their current practices. Conceivably, our onlookers want to know whether students will benefit from and need such instruction, and, if so, how best to transact current practices and staff capacities and confidence to ensure optimum realization of any such changes.

Survey data from our study revealed that most students recognized a need for academic English-language skills in their daily studies and future study plans. They identified difficulties students had in fulfilling effectively the academic tasks of writing, oral presentation, and reading. They were not confident about their academic English-language proficiency in these three aspects and a great majority welcomed the prospect of EAP instruction that is oriented to prepare them better for future academic courses where English is the MOI. Qualitative data from the focus group interviews indicate an imperative for EAP's introduction as the step to be taken beyond the nation's current pause at the decision threshold. Both instructors and students agreed that EAP is needed and that its introduction would be timely in complementing the current College English programs to better address students' needs. However, these data also cautioned that any such step should be taken in ways mindful of the practical matters that will need to be thoroughly considered and addressed. Students and instructors alike anticipated that it will be a great challenge to current College English program design and implementation, and to people and resources of the academic departments who manage the responsibilities of adaptation, to implement such a new component in ways aimed to meet the expectations of such a large number of students.

From this case study, we have formed an optimistic conclusion in finding that opportunities and challenges coexist in negotiating appropriate EAP practices in Chinese universities. On the one hand, students feel a strong need for some preparatory courses to help get them ready for English MOI academic courses at junior or senior years. Meanwhile, we see that in implementing EAP practices in Chinese EFL contexts, two major challenges are to be overcome. The first is the size of the student population in China. Typical western EAP practices, though very welcome, are available to students of only a limited number of colleges. To meet the demands of such large numbers of students, more practical models are to be cultivated. The hybrid models of Fudan University and Tsinghua University might be an option. Another challenge lies in the pragmatics of responsibility in implementing EAP. If EAP is to be introduced as a new component to the current College English provision, instructors will face a new round of reform about which there are some reservations in their readiness to commit. This is not unexpected, given much the same conditions of resistance reported by Zhang et al. (2011). Suggestions about possibilities for collaboration and cooperative efforts between academic instructors and College English teachers that have been provided by instructors in the focus group interview of this study will shed light on the resolution of this complicated yet urgent issue. Their contributions, along with those of the students in our study, reinforce the potential and positivity of stakeholders' voices being recognized, accessed, and incorporated into the considerations and decisions that lie ahead for policy makers and administrators when launching nationwide English education reforms.

ACKNOWLEDGEMENTS

We would like to thank our colleagues from the College English Section at Peking University for their help with the surveys and focus group interviews, and the students who participated in the focus group interviews for their cooperation. Our thanks also go to the anonymous reviewers and editors for valuable comments and suggestions.

REFERENCES

Alexander, O., Argent, S., & Spencer, J. (2008). *EAP essentials: A teacher's guide to principles and practice*. Reading, UK: Garnet.

Bartlett, B. J., & Piggot-Irvine, E. (2008). What is evaluating action research? In E. Piggot-Irvine & B. J. Bartlett (Eds.), *Evaluating action research* (pp. 9-52). Auckland, New Zealand: NZCER Press.

Cai, J. G. (2010). Quan yingyu jiaoxue kexingxing yanjiu [The feasibility study of EMI: A case analysis of Public Relation course of Fudan]. *Foreign Languages in China, 7*(6), 61-67.

Cai, J. G. (2011a). CBI lilun kuangjia xia de fenke yingyu jiaoxue [Exploring disciplinary-based English teaching on the basis of CBI (Content-based Instruction)]. *Foreign Language Education, 5*, 39-42.

Cai, J. G. (2011b). Ningbo nuodinghan daxue he fudan daxue de daxue yigyu jiaoxue moshi chayi bijiao [Contrastive study on English teaching models between The University of Nottingham Ningbo, China (UNNC) and Fudan University]. *China University Teaching, 1*(19-23).

Cai, J. G. (2012a). "Xueshu yingyu" kecheng xuqiu fenxi he jiaoxue fangfa yanjiu [EAP needs analysis and the study on teaching methodology]. *Foreign Language Learning Theory and Practice, 2*, 30-35.

Cai, J. G. (2012b). Zonghe yingyu haishi xueshu yingyu. (Sharing views on general English teaching reform). *Journal of Northeast Normal University (Philosophy and Social Sciences), 1*, 94-96.

Cai, J. G., & Liao, L. Z. (2010a). ELE haishi ESP: lun woguo daxue yingyu fazhan fangxiang. (ELE vs. ESP--the Orientation of College English). *Computer-Assisted Foreign Language Education, 135*(9), 20-26.

Cai, J. G., & Liao, L. Z. (2010b). Xueshu yingyu haishi zhuanye yingyu – woguo daxue ESP jiaoxue chongxin dingwei sikao [EAP vs. ESP – The orientation of college English]. *Foreign Language Education, 6*, 47-50.

Department of Higher Education of Ministry of Education of the People's Republic of China. (2004). *College English curriculum requirements (for trial implementation)*. Shanghai, China: Shanghai Foreign Education Press.

Etherington, S. (2005). *Innovation in the assessment of English for academic purposes*. Unpublished project report. University of Salford. Salford, UK. Retrieved from http://usir.salford.ac.uk/2021/2/etherington0304.pdf

Evans, S. (2003). Hong Kong's new English language policy in education. *World Englishes, 19*(2), 185-204.

Gill, S. K., & Kirkpatrick, A. (2013). English in Asian and European higher education. In C. A. Chapelle (Ed.), *The encyclopedia of applied linguistics* (1st ed., pp. 1916-1920). Oxford, UK: Blackwell Publishing Ltd.

Hudson, P. (2009). Learning to teach science using English as the medium of instruction. *Eurasia Journal of Mathematics, Science & Technology Education, 5*(2), 165-170.

Hyland, K. (2006). *English for academic purposes: An advanced resource book*. New York: Routledge.

Hyland, K., & Hamp-Lyons, L. (2002). EAP: Issues and directions. *Journal of English for Academic Purposes, 1*(1), 1-12.

Jiang, Y. C., & Li, N. (2010). Guonei zhuanmen yongtu yingyu yanjiu 20 nian: huigu yu sikao [Review and reflection on domestic ESP research in the past two decades]. *Journal of Ningbo University, 32*(2), 104-109.

Jordan, R. R. (1997). *English for academic purposes: A guide and resource book for teachers*. Cambrdge, UK: Cambridge University Press.

Ju, Y. M. (2006). Guowai EAP jiaoxue yu yanjiu gailan [EAP teaching and research abroad]. *Foreign Language Education, 27*(2), 1-6.

Ministry of Education of the People's Republic of China. (2001). *Jiaoyubu guanyu jiji tuijin xiaoxue kaishe yingyu kecheng de zhidao yijian* [MOE guidelines for actively promoting the offering of English classes in elementary schools]. Retrieved from http://www.gov.cn/gongbao/content/2001/content_61196.htm.

Qin, X. B. (2003). ESP de xingzhi, fanchou he jiaoxue yuanze [The nature, scope and principles of ESP teaching]. *Journal of South China University of Technology, 5*(4), 79-83.

Sultan, S., Borland, H., & Eckersley, B. (2012, July 4). *English as medium of instruction (EMI) in Indonesia public junior secondary school: Students' language use, attitudes/motivation and foreign language outcomes*. Paper presented at the ACTA International TESOL Conference, Cairns, Australia.

Sun, J., & Xu, B. (2012). Discussion on the factors influencing the effect of bilingual teaching in Chinese universities and countermeasures. *Higher Education of Social Science, 2*(3), 27-31.

Wen, Q. F., & Hu, W. Z. (2007). History and policy of English education in Mainland China. In H. C. Yeon & B. Spolsky (Eds.), *English education in Asia: History and policies* (pp. 1-31). Seoul, Korea: Asia TEFL.

Xia, J. M. (2003). *Foreign language course design: Modern theory and practice*. Shanghai, China: Shanghai Foreign Language Education Press.

Yang, H. Z. (2010). *EAP zai zhongguo: huigu, xianzhuang yu zhanwang* [EAP in China: Retrospect, state of arts and prospect]. Paper presented at the Chinese ESP Forum, Beijing, China.

Yao, L. (2001). Guowai zhuanye yongtu yingyu pingjie [An overview of EAP practices in the world]. *Foreign Language Teaching Abroad, 3*, 9-14.

Yu, L. M., & Yuan, D. P. (2005). Shuangyu jiaoxue yu daxue yingyu jiaoxue gaige [Bilingual education and college English teaching reform]. *Higher Education Research, 26*(3), 74-78.

Zhang, C. X. (2006). Australia Wollongong daxue "xueshu yingyu" kecheng jiaoxue moshi [EAP teaching at University of Wollongong in Australia]. *Journal of PLA University of Foreign Languages, 29*(4), 48-51.

Zhang, W. M., Zhang, W. X., & Liu, M. H. (2011). Tongyong yingyu jiaoxue zhuanxiang xueshu yingyu jiaoxue de taisuo [From EGP to EAP-Proposal for College English reform at Tsinghua University]. *Foreign Language Research, 129*(5), 11-14.

Zhang, X. J. (2004). Yingguo EAP jiaoxue fazhan dui gongwai yanjiusheng yingyu kecheng shezhi de qifa [Inspiration of UK EAP practices for graduate English course design]. *Journal of Sichuan International Studies University, 20*(6), 152-155.

Zhu, Y. M. (2006). Luomaniya EAP jiaoxue taolun ke tanxi [Exploring the Romanian EAP seminars]. *Journal of Human Business College, 13*(2), 126-128.

Yanmei Gao
Institute of Linguistics and Applied Linguistics
School of Foreign Languages
Peking University, China

Brendan Bartlett
Learning Sciences Institute Australia
Australian Catholic University
Brisbane, Australia

HINA ASHRAF, LUQMAN HAKIM & IRUM ZULFIQAR

3. ENGLISH FOR ACADEMIC PURPOSES IN PLURILINGUAL PAKISTAN

INTRODUCTION

Pakistan, which became a separate state after gaining independence from Britain in 1947, is located in a diverse multilingual and plurilingual region of South Asia. Its linguistic diversity on the Greenberg index is measured to be 0.762, which, were it 1, would imply no two people in the country have the same first or heritage language (Lewis, 2009). Studies suggest the local linguistic repertoire of Pakistan is inherently plurilingual (Canagarajah & Ashraf, 2013) and new forms of globalization have made English part of this plurilingual repertoire (Canagarajah, 2009; Canagarajah & Ashraf, 2013). English, as the official language, and Urdu, as the national language and lingua franca, are dominant in official and educational settings. Until recently, the medium of instruction (MOI) in Pakistan was predominantly Urdu. In the last two decades, however, a popular shift to English MOI from early school to higher education began to take place (Ashraf, 2008). The New Education Policy (NEP) of the Pakistan's Ministry of Education (2009) reinforces English-medium education and requires all research to be documented in English for wider access. Owing to these literacy demands and global trends, programs of English for academic and communicative purposes are being added increasingly to the college and university curriculum. In this chapter, we emphasize that the codes mandated in ideologically monolingual educational environments aspired to by English for Academic Purposes (EAP) (and the NEP) are in effect problematized by the local plurilingual social and institutional settings.

English for Academic Purposes in Pakistan

Though English has been used in the Indian subcontinent and its educational systems for more than 200 years, the language education policy in Pakistan has not been explicit until recently. The long-term policy goal was to have Urdu as the MOI at secondary, tertiary, and higher education levels (Mansoor, 2004; Ministry of Education, 1959). Yet from the earliest education policy documents in Pakistan, English was maintained as the MOI in higher education (Ministry of Education, 1959). For most of the period after Independence, Urdu was officially the MOI for Grades 1-12 and, despite occasional shifts to English, the predominant code for all classroom registers, including the discourse and lexis across school subjects, particularly in public sector institutions (Ashraf, 2008). According to the NEP, study of English is now to be introduced in schools from the primary level along

I. Liyanage & T. Walker (eds.), English for Academic Purposes (EAP) in Asia, 33–49.
© *2014 Sense Publishers. All rights reserved.*

with Urdu and a regional language. It is also recommended as the MOI from Grade 4 onwards and compulsory from Grade 6 (Ministry of Education, 2009, p. 20). The policy declares that after completion of Grade 12, learners of English as a second language are expected to be proficient users of the language, possessing effective listening, speaking, reading, and writing skills (Ministry of Education, 2009). The Higher Education Commission (HEC; previously known as the University Grants Commission – UGC) recommends all higher education instruction to be in English, except for some subjects of humanities for which English-language resources are not available. The implications of using English MOI in higher education, as Schleppegrell and O'Hallaron (2011, p. 4) note, cannot be ignored: "learning to read, write, and interact using academic language requires support for language development that assists students in engaging with the communicative and literacy demands of disciplinary learning." Given a lack of trained English-language teachers, limited resources, and students' familial backgrounds and education, such support has been largely absent and the transition from Urdu or local language MOI to English MOI in higher education has not yet been achieved.

Research from Pakistani schools suggested that, even in those using English as the MOI, students are taught in a local language, and assessed in English (Canagarajah & Ashraf, 2013; Mansoor, 2005; Rahman, 2002; Shamim, 2008, 2011). Although students are assessed using English only, in textbooks English is interspersed with Urdu terminology, translation, and explanation. Reliance on Urdu was also reflected in pedagogical practices in higher education in the traditional English programs (e.g. Master of Arts) in classical British English literature and canonical prose; for learning, students tended to rely on the translated versions of texts yet were examined in English (for details, see Rahman, 2001). Such practices are forms of translanguaging, a term originally translated from Welsh, *rawsieithu* referring to a pedagogical practice in bilingual classes in which input is provided in one language and tasks are performed in another (Cenoz & Gorter, 2011). The scope of this term has now broadened to refer to a process, a naturally occurring phenomenon in communicative practices of multilinguals (Canagarajah, 2009, 2011), and the norm in multilingual countries (García, 2009), involving multiple discursive practices, that is, "a systematic shift from one language to the other for specific reasons" (Coyle, Hood, & Marsh, 2010, p. 16) with "no clear cut borders between the languages of bilinguals" (García, 2009, p. 47). Notwithstanding, the NEP aims to separate English from local languages in higher education to designate it as the language to be used for academic purposes. To address this requirement of English MOI, the HEC has, therefore, in the past few years taken an aggressive approach to create more learning spaces for English that risks systematic weakening of Urdu and other local languages.

HEC's English Language Teaching Reforms project (ELTR) was an attempt to bridge the gap between the MOI of schools and universities, and to address the dissatisfaction of students and teachers with available English-language resources (Higher Education Commission Pakistan, 2009). A National Committee on English (NCE) was formed in 2003 to address declining standards of English-language teaching in educational institutions (see Higher Education Commission Pakistan,

2009). Following the NCE recommendations, ELTR designed new curricula for English-language and EAP teachers. To enhance opportunities for students and teachers to use English as the MOI, ELTR also designed pedagogical courses for teachers of EAP. These courses match Gillett's (2004) description of EAP, that is, "the language and associated skills that students need to undertake study in higher education through the medium of English." HEC interventions to support English MOI, therefore, led to formulation of EAP courses such as Communication Skills in English, Functional English, Technical Writing, and Business Communication, the prescribed curricula of which are made available to educational institutions through HEC. These courses are now compulsory in undergraduate degree programs, and aim to support students' academic research skills in postgraduate English-medium programs. In the first year, for example, university students are taught to communicate in English only and use English for performing various functions such as making requests, writing job applications, and reporting experiments. In the second and subsequent years, these courses are centered on English for Specific Purposes (ESP) and academic writing in different disciplines, aiming to develop students' proficiency and performance in core subject areas. Teacher training and capacity-building workshops for university teachers, presented by local experts and international consultants, are also conducted by ELTR on a regular basis. Ideally, this array of initiatives would create English MOI classrooms that enable students to meet the academic goals of university education and research. Yet the languages and repertoire of the local linguistic landscape impact significantly on the goals of English MOI and EAP in Pakistan. In the next section we describe plurilingual practices, and their influence on development of English-language skills.

Plurilingual Practices and English Proficiency

In Pakistan, along with socialization into a regional language (e.g., Punjabi, Sindhi, Pashto, etc.), and the lingua franca, Urdu, the 96% Muslim population is taught some basic Arabic for religious scriptures and prayers (see Canagarajah & Ashraf, 2013; Rahman, 2002). In addition to English as the official language and medium of education, English meshed with Urdu in plurilingual mass media communication is not foreign to the people in general. In this section, we deconstruct these communicative patterns to provide the context in which Pakistani EAP programs function.

Research on plurilingual Urdu and English practices in Pakistan suggests that plurilingual communicative patterns bring new identities to speakers (Canagarajah & Ashraf, 2013; Rahman, 2009). In the South Asian tradition of plurilingualism and multilingualism, attitudes and strategies of Pakistani speakers create such fluidity that there are very few breaks in communication (Canagarajah, 2009; Canagarajah & Ashraf, 2013; Pattanayak, 1984; Rahman, 2002, 2011). The speakers do not just move from one language to the other, nor do they treat these languages as monolingual codes; rather, they draw from them as one linguistic repertoire (Canagarajah, 2009, 2013; see also García, 2009, 2011), accessing "a

35

languaging continuum" (García, 2009, p. 47) without attempts to establish proficiency in both languages. The examples and data presented in this chapter show similar characteristics. Moreover, the examples we present here are what individuals, irrespective of educational background, come across in their everyday lives in the Pakistani linguistic landscape.

The official endorsements on local currency notes, which mesh English and Urdu, establish for the layperson the official co-existence of both languages. District-level offices in Pakistan function in Urdu (and also Sindhi in the southern province of Sindh), while federal offices and bureaucracy function in English (Rahman, 2002). The presence of both languages leads to mixing of plurilingual codes at various levels. The strategies of borrowing and mixing become common normative and cultural practices over a period of time. Annamalai (2001), describing plurilingual communication, argues that integrated loan words and borrowings from other languages are treated in their own unique styles by local speakers, thus making all codes part of a single system drawn on at will.

The language choices made in marketing often demonstrate creative forms of translanguaging. A fruit juice seller's use of original scripts, transliteration, and translation to advertise his kiosk is a good example of such practice where, *Fresh Fruit Juice Corner*, followed by *Strawberry Milkshake* in English, is transliterated into Urdu. The target audience would find it easy to follow English concepts in Urdu script, yet the more familiar vocabulary, the names of the fruits, that is, mango, apple, and peach, are Urdu, both words and script. Another example is the language used in advertising a cellular network package in print media. Terms like *Lifestyle, Happy Hour, 'Uuummm'* and *'Sounds Great'* are embedded into the Urdu text in the advertisement, while the syntax of the two is meshed: 'See what happens, *when you zem it!*'. Similarly words like *free* and *calls* are transliterated into Urdu.

The hybrid syntax in the examples, above, meshes both codes into one. Moreover, it does not affect the meaning-making process in the interactions. Rather, meanings are negotiated implicitly or explicitly (Littlejohn, 2008; Slimani, 2001) in an interaction of English with the regional languages and, especially in the urban areas, Urdu. In plurilingual contexts, according to Canagarajah (2009, p. 10), meaning and intelligibility are intersubjective in participants' interaction:

> The participants in an interaction produce meaning and accomplish their communicative objectives in relation to their purposes and interests. In this sense, meaning is socially constructed. Meaning does not reside in the language; it is produced in practice.

Plurilingual communicative patterns negotiate space in multilingual social contexts, and, from a linguistic point of view, they present fascinating meshing of syntax, vocabulary, translation, and transliteration of languages. Yet in the social context of Pakistan, these practices, on the one hand, establish the hegemony of English in public domains, while on the other, they also negotiate its space in what once would be considered the sole domain of Urdu. Plurilingual communicative trends beset EAP with challenges, particularly as knowledge transfer is proposed to be monolingual and in standard academic English.

METHOD

In this section we present data from an experimental study in which students responded orally to three audio texts recorded in English, Urdu, and code-mixed English-Urdu in order to determine their response language as monolingual or plurilingual. A set of 108 students, 54 males and 54 females, enrolled in higher secondary schools and undergraduate and postgraduate programs responded orally to audio recordings of three different text types – narrative, expository and instructional – each in a different code, that is, English-only, Urdu-only, and English-Urdu mixed. Considering the MOI effect on students' proficiency, an equal number of students from both English- and Urdu-medium school backgrounds were selected. To avoid "the potential carry-over effect" (Mecartty, 2001, p. 273) the sequencing for the text-type and language code was changed for each student. To meet these required methodological requirements, the Graeco-Latin Square was used for the design.[1] Students were provided brief information on the audio texts before the interaction with them began, and following exposure to each audio text, students were asked to recount what they heard. The responses did not bear the same orientation of text types as students negotiated information in their answers. This has been illustrated in the next section. A total of 324 (108 x 3) responses were recorded and transcribed for analysis (for more detailed information and description of the process readers are referred to Hakim, 2010).

FINDINGS AND DISCUSSION

From the outset it is important to note that, though students heard two monolingual codes and one mixed, the preferred response code was mixed; of the 324 responses only 90 were monolingual, and the remaining plurilingual in the mixed English-Urdu code (see Table 1). Monolingual responses in English were more frequent (75) compared to those in Urdu (15), indexing those students' identities with the ideological English experience of EAP programs. It was also interesting to note that no student responded in only Urdu to the English audio-text, whereas 9 students selected English as their response language to the Urdu audio-text. With the increased emphasis on EAP programs in educational institutions, these English responses indicate their preferred identities. Fifty-two students responded in English only to the English texts, but only 13 responded in Urdu to the Urdu texts.

In the 234 plurilingual responses, English and Urdu codes mesh in varied patterns with no demonstration of advanced proficiency in either of these languages. Table 2 shows a significant difference between the means of variation when the input language is in the mixed code (mean=13.89) as compared to Urdu

Table 1. Response language and input language

Response Language	Input Language			Total
	English	Urdu	Mixed	
English monolingual	52	9	14	75
Urdu monolingual	0	13	2	15
Mixed	56	86	92	234
	108	108	108	324

Table 2. Means of number of codeswitches

Input Language	Mean	N	Std. Deviation
English	6.38	108	9.066
Urdu	7.32	108	6.623
Mixed	13.89	108	9.750
Total	9.20	324	9.189

(7.32) or English (6.38). The results support the notion that the code in which students hear the talk has a strong influence on their performance. At the same time the results indicate that despite the fact that English is the students' second language, students tend to mesh English in the mixed codes so that most of the time it appears as if they are having a conversation in English (Rahman, 2009). Their responses to the monolingual texts demonstrate a similar inclination. They include more English words in their speech even when they are responding to monolingual Urdu texts, and a majority of them do not respond in English when they hear an English text, and prefer the mixed code. However, their mixing does not show any consistent patterns. This frequency of mixed responses/ translanguaging demonstrates challenges to monolingual EAP programs.

According to Blommaert (2010, p. 246) we live in a multilingual complex of communicative practices in which many varieties, styles, genres, accents and codes occur in the "moment-to-moment evolving variation between varieties of language." To follow the variation patterns in students' communication, we subjected the responses to a corpus analysis. We first studied the synchronic variation within these responses by examining how the codes were mixed in the concordances. The data demonstrated that learners relied on Urdu words mostly in the use of function words. Peculiar was the use of *and*, translated as *aur* in Urdu, sequencing devices, and *in*, that is, *mey*, in Urdu. Below we discuss their usages in different contexts as students shuttled between the English and Urdu codes.

Use of Additional and Sequencing Devices

Though both are used interchangeably, *aur* is more frequent in the responses to the audio texts as compared to its English equivalent *and*. *Aur* was used in 469 instances compared to 303 uses of *and*. In the mixed responses, *aur* was used 190 times, while *and* occurred only 22 times. The pattern of usage also varied. In English, *and* has been employed only as a linking word and as an additional device, while in Urdu the functions are multiple: It is used as an addition word, for sequencing of events and instructions, as a transitional device expressing a new thought, and even for taking a pause. In learners' English responses its use was more frequent in response to instructional and expository texts, while in Urdu responses its use spread across all the three text types.

And has been used for sequencing in the instructional audio texts wherein most replies used the Urdu equivalent of *after this* or *next*, that is, *uskē baad (transcribed as uskay baad)* and *aur phir*. Responses were also frequented by *then*, for which the Urdu equivalents are *tau* and *phir ūs mey*.

For more clarity on variations in the use of *and/aur* as sequencing device, we here describe the instructional texts and responses to them in further detail. The responses to the instructional text did not just illustrate an absence of the transitional devices, but also of the action verbs themselves. Table 3 presents the overall characteristics of the instructional texts.

Table 3. Characteristics of the instructional texts

English	Urdu	Mixed English-Urdu
Flight safety instructions	Directs how to prepare soap	Stepwise recipe for preparing kebabs
Imperatives/first form of verb	Imperatives/first form of verb Adverb of time Third person pronoun	First person pronoun Imperative/directive/first form of verb Conjunction "and"
Action verbs "fasten," "pull," "close," "insert," "cover," etc.	Action verbs "dalain," "helain," etc. Linking words "abb," "tu," "jabb," etc.	Action verbs "mix karain," "laga dain," "paka lain," etc.

Thirty-six students listened to each of the instructional texts, yet the concordances did not demonstrate the presence of the action verbs in the responses. This exhibits a rather peculiar attitude to their usage as Figures 1-4, below, illustrate.

N	Concordance
1	is going to take off, everyone should fasten his or her seat-belts and if there
2	would announce that everyone should fasten his seat-belts properly. In case of
3	First of all we will...jo hy... fasten the seat belts. Ah...put on the
4	I listen that we should fasten our seat belt in case of
5	Ah...you should fasten your seat belts. First the main
6	Ah.....we should fasten our seat-belts. It helps and...ah...
7	and can also help them and you have to fasten your seat belt first and the
8	first instruction was that be seated and fasten your seat belt. And then any gas
9	Fasten your sea- belts and ...ah... fasten your seat-belts and agr
10	Fasten your sea- belts and
11	Ah ...first of all you to fasten your seat-belt. Whein you are
12	that first of all you have to fasten your seat-belt. You have to
13	Fasten your seat belt and if in
14	oxygen mask is dropped and fasten it on your mouth and in
15	precautions say/included that fasten your seat belts... and... check
16	tu ap jo hy apna seat-belt jo hy wo apna fasten kar lein. Usko bandhain. Aur
17	to save yourself. Ah...you have to ah...fasten...you have to tight seat-belt.
18	Ok...while you are in a plane first ...ah...fasten your seat-belts. And while
19	I listened that first of all you have to fasten the seat-belt. And ...in case of

Figure 1. Concordances "fasten" (Image from Wordsmith 5.0)

Each of these figures illustrates the use of action verbs by the students in either of the languages. For example, of the 36 responses to English flight safety instructions, *fasten* appeared in only 19 concordances, while its Urdu equivalent, *baandh* (also translated as *bandh*, with the accent variation), occurred only 7 times. Overall, not all students referred to fastening seat belts, which was the main instruction given to passengers. For inserting the safely buckle in the belt, only one student out of 36 used the word *insert*. We looked for its Urdu equivalent, *dalein*, but came across that usage only in responses to the other two instructional texts: 2 of 36 students used it in responses to mixed-code instructions for preparing kebabs; one student used the word in response to the Urdu instructions for preparing soap.

N	Concordance
1	karta hy ya land kr raha ho tu seat-belt bandh lein kion keh ek damm jatka agr
2	sar kay saat saheeh tareeqay sey baandh lein ta keh hadsaat ya kisi aur
3	mey betnay sey pehlay apni beloun ko bandh lein. Ussay yae hota hy keh
4	tu aap apni hefaazat kay liay seat-belt baandh lein. Dusra yae...aur unhoun
5	kr lein. Aur plastic band jo hy uss sey bandh lein. Aur dusroun ki madad krain.
6	safety-belt jo hota hy wo saheeh krkay bandh lein. Ess kay elawa jo mask hota
7	aur take off kay waqt apnay seat-belts bandh kay raknay chaheay. Aur agr

Figure 2. Concordances "baandh/bandh" (Image from Wordsmith 5.0)

N	Concordance	Set
1	fry karnay hien. Phir ess mey namak dalain, merchain daalain. Namak	
2	yae hy keh sabb sey pehlay thail dalain karhai mey. Usko garm karain.	
3	ne kaha keh usmay thory sey lai dalain.. aur usko tabb tak mix karain	

Figure 3. Concordances "dalein" (Image from Wordsmith 5.0)

N	Concordance
1	procedure you ah... buckle...ah... you...insert the buckle in belt. If you

Figure 4. Concordance "insert" (Image from Wordsmith 5.0)

We next examined the trends of translanguaging in students' responses. The following illustrations, (1) and (2) below, demonstrate how students draw on resources from both languages as they negotiate information.

Interviewer: How would you demonstrate the safety features and procedures in a plane as you heard them in the cassette?

(1)   *Aa* ... precautionary measures have been told ... ah ... how to protect yourself while you are sitting in a plane. And if there is some threat of danger ... how to save yourself. *Aa* ... you have to ah ... fasten ... you have to tight seat belt. Here you have oxygen mask ... up there any *aa* ... any threat ... or incident are going to happen. How you would save yourself. This is discussed in this cassette.

(2)   You have to fasten your seat belts ... ah ... in case of emergency ... ah ... *oxygen ka jo* mask *hy, wo baher rakhain ap. Jab* take off *ho raha hota hy tab be rakhain* on. In case of aircraft *mey koi kharabi ho tu* fasten your seat belts and move towards door. And take off your shoes ... or high heels shoes.

(You have to fasten your seat belts in case of emergency. That oxygen mask, keep it outside. When the plane is taking off, keep it on even then. In case of emergency in the aircraft, fasten your seat belts and move towards the door. And take off your shoes or high heels.)

In (1) the focus is more on what information the student has heard, and it appears to be an effort in recall more than in demonstrating the instruction. On the other hand, in the response in the mixed code (2), *fasten* appears twice. *Take off* is used twice as well, however, its use varies in both instances. The first is with reference to the plane, where it is combined with "*jab*" and "*ho raha ho*" to imply *when it is taking off*. The second is the instruction to take off one's shoes or high heels in case of emergency. This again hints at South Asian plurilingual practices as described by Canagarajah (2009), of speakers constructing their own norms rather than

41

moving towards someone else's target language. Speakers create their own norms and rise to their own challenges in each situation. The meshing of the codes is also evident in the syntactic structure of (2). In the first part of this utterance, the verb clause is in English (*You have to fasten your seat belts*), while the second is in Urdu (*oxygen ka jo mask hy wo bahar rakein*, that is, *keep the oxygen mask outside*). It continues to be Urdu until the third sentence, where from English it moves to Urdu, to shuttle back to English in the last two instructions. These translanguaging practices, as Annamalai (2001) argues, cannot be considered codeswitches as the respondents do not appear to distinguish between the codes as separate languages. This particular orientation to the communicative practices in the students' responses sometimes lends a pidgin-like character to the mixed code.

Use of mey/in

In the case of *in/mey*, students meshed these into Urdu and English clauses for varied and creative purposes. In the mixed responses, *in* appeared 129 times, while there were 478 instances of *mey*. The collocates include opening statements, for example, *In this cassette, In case of, In front of you, Es mey ye bataaya gaya hae* (This [reference to the audio cassette] tells us that), and *Aur es mey* (And in this [reference to the audio cassette]). *Mey* has also been used in translation of English collocates that use *for*. Below we present some examples of *in* used in mixed-code responses.

(3)   wo insha'Allah progress karay ga <u>in</u> the next coming years.

With the Will of God he will progress in the coming years.

(4)   There should not be left anyone <u>in</u> the karahi. And after they are mixed nicely put laai <u>in</u> them.

Nothing should be left in the wok. And after they are mixed nicely, add the paste.

(5)   Twenty-third March k din they all gathered <u>in</u> Lahore.

On (the day of) 23rd March they all gathered in Lahore.

(6)   Thirteen per cent life kamm ho jati hy if smoking karnay sey. Plus yae hy keh ek cigarette mey twenty ... ek pack mey twenty cigarettes hotey hein, which is sufficient which could cause cancer. Secondly ... ek young age mey agr cancers diagnose ho jaiy. Tu it would be easy to treat him. Aur ... yae hy keh keh jo cigarettes hein ess sey lung cancer ho jata hy.

With smoking life decreases by 13%. Plus one packet of cigarettes has twenty of them, which is sufficient to lead to cancer. Secondly, cancer may be easy to diagnose while young. Thus it would be easier to treat him. And with cigarettes lung cancer is caused.

In each of the above, *in* is used in a different context. It refers to a future time, to adding an ingredient, and to gathering in a place. This mixing, however, lends a distinct character to the utterances. The shifts in the syntax and the overall structure are sometimes unidiomatic. In (3), the first part of the utterance is in Urdu syntax with *progress* inserted in the clause: *Wo insha'Allah* (If God Wills) and *keray ga* (he will) are Urdu phrases. The second part of (3), *in the coming years*, is entirely in English and so is the syntax. In (4), *karahi* and *laai* are Urdu words. In most responses *mey* is used with English nouns and verbs, but from (4) it becomes clear that there are no stable patterns that would guarantee consistent usage. Similarly, in (5), Urdu syntax for the first part of the utterance shifts to English in the second part. In the final example, (6), variation in syntax, insertion of English and Urdu words in the syntax of the other languages, and breaks in the utterance are affected by the weak grammar structure. The speaker in (6) begins in English, with Urdu insertions with the flow of thought. This is followed by continual shifts from syntax of one language to the other. These switches appear automatic and do not affect the flow of the thought. Similarly, note the use of sequencing devices, *plus* and *secondly*, followed by *aur* in the last sentence. In this instance, the grammatical structure is weaker, but the mixing is not affected.

Though sustained patterns of translanguaging are not easily identifiable in the responses, the plurilingual repertoires of these students share certain similar characteristics. Their responses demonstrate that students negotiate meaning by drawing from resources in both the languages. Their cognitive processing entails shifts in syntactical patterns, and vocabulary. Yet the overall analysis exhibits students' comfort level in the plurilingualism they find in their social environment. In the following section, we discuss the implications of above findings for EAP programs in Pakistan.

EAP in Plurlingual Pakistan

Similar to other studies in multilingual contexts, in the current study, translanguaging in the participants' responses appeared an unbidden, natural phenomenon (Bhatia & Ritchie, 2004; Canagarajah, 2011). Though not encouraged by the interviewer, the presence of a code-mixed text allowed for students to negotiate their preferred code in the responses. However, such plurilingual competence is a resource that clashes with the policy goals of EAP programs in Pakistan, which mandate teaching, and in turn demanding from students, a prestige variety of academic English (see also Moyer & Martín Rojo, 2007). In multilingual countries, such as Pakistan, the standard variety of English is visualized, particularly in higher education, as an *ideological monoglot phenomenon* (Silverstein, 1996) resting on the belief that a society essentially bears monolingual characters, and which denies multilingual backgrounds and linguistic diversity (Blommaert, 2010; Blommaert & Verschueren, 1998). The caveat in Pakistani plurilingual contexts, and similar EAP programs, is that monoglot ideologies are embedded in social and academic contexts where instead translanguaging is becoming the norm.

Institutes of higher education follow the HEC's English language curriculum guidelines, which focus on fostering communication skills and academic publishing. Yet EAP programs in higher education entail content different from that in earlier secondary school and tertiary education curricula of English, that comprised anthologies of essays, short stories, poems, and one-act plays. In the school curriculum, students learn *about* English grammar through its conventions and rules, but not its use in context. To achieve par with global standards, EAP courses introduce learners to the dominant Anglo-American writing patterns and academic discourses, and students' success depends on how well they appropriate those conventions in their own practices (Schleppegrell & O'Hallaron, 2011). The shift in the pedagogical focus at higher education levels also affects their skills of transferring knowledge (Mansoor, Hussain, Sikandar, & Ahsa, 2009). In our study, this was illustrated in the negotiation of information as participants responded to questions on the texts (see excerpts, above).

Khubchandani (2008) argues that in plurilingual societies, and particularly for education, the need to standardize languages is crucial. The existence of monoglot ideology in the Pakistani system, and in its top-down policy of education, may be sustained not only because Urdu and other local languages are becoming inherently weak, but also because, as Mohanty (2010, p. 150) argues in the context of Indian plurilingualism, in the official positioning of languages "they are weakened systematically and cumulatively by prolonged exclusion from socially and economically significant domains including education." Translanguaging allows speakers to index their identity with the languages that empower social discourse. It brings the speakers close to the idealized variety of English, and in turn offers better access to resources. Unlike other communities in which ethnic differences are preserved through languages, in South Asian countries languages also help maintain overarching community identity with other groups (Canagarajah, 2009). In this case, plurilingual practices foster new forms of identity aligned with an English-speaking community, and Westernized percept. Plurilingual English in Pakistan sets the norms for the majority of students who do not have access to elite English schools that take pride in English being the sole MOI and mode of communication (Rahman, 2002, 2009). On the other hand, in the appropriation of codes, most learners negotiate norms for functioning in the target language and their terms for communicating with the knowledge domains. These practices undermine the goals of monolithic English programs.

Given learners' backgrounds of multilingual social and academic cultures, plurilingual practices in academic settings become inevitable, and even unconscious, and, as illustrated in our findings, learners appear to be hampered by their limited English proficiency. As a result, in our roles of instructors and facilitators, we are compelled to create space for Urdu in the classrooms in accordance with the proficiency levels of the students and their plurilingual communicative repertoire. Most of the time this space is confined to student discussion, but the journey from plurilingual discourse to the monolingual English required in EAP courses is not easy. Instructors acknowledge the unpreparedness of students who, although trained for 12 to 14 years to attain proficiency in English, then find it difficult to meet the demands of English-medium programs in higher education (Zulfiqar, 2012). In a set of focus-group interviews with students, Zulfiqar (2012, p. 196) indicates the need of taking into consideration students' perspectives of their linguistic ability as it is shaped by the plurilingual repertoire:

[W]e learnt enough to get something … *Hum understand kerletē hain* but the problem is that *hum kaheen beth ker sehi tarha* deliver *nahi ker saktē* [...].

Ma'am, *aik aur baat yh hai k jo … larkē jab is* field *mey a jatē hein,* engineering *mey,* medical *me,y ya isi tarha jab unko apni manzil mil jaati hai, tou woh* English *ko aik* secondary subject *k tor per lena shuru ker dete hein. Keh jitni* English *seekhni thi woh hum seekh chukē hain … Agar hamein nahi aati, tou theeek hai ab hamein saari zindagi nahi seekh saktē [...]*

(Madam, we have learned [the language] enough to understand some thing. We do understand; however, the problem is we cannot deliver while being a part of discussion.) [...] [W]hen boys join the field of engineering for study, or medicine, or any other field like this, they somehow achieve their goal. They consider English as a secondary subject believing that they have learnt it enough, and all that they could. And in case if they couldn't (learn it), it strengthens their belief that they can't learn it for the rest of life [...]

The student is not confident to speak in English only, and he is perplexed that there is any requirement for the English language once he is enrolled in the engineering program. In his struggle to communicate in English, the student shuttles between plurilingual practices and monolingual expectations of the socio-academic environment of Pakistan. If higher education classrooms in Pakistan were functionally multilingual, expectations of complementation and formal convergence of grammar in various language forms (García, 2009) would be accepted as instances of creativity and intelligibility (Canagarajah, 2009, 2011). However, in the current policy context, these practices are considered interference problems, or even errors, that assume forms of language disability when learners apply their language skills to advanced-level tasks to meet the requirements of EAP programs. Yet the big challenges for practitioners are the constant shifts in codes and syntax, and the hampered and confused responses of plurilingual students, which lend a pidgin-like character to their English-language skills. The multilingual and multiethnic backgrounds of students and teachers, along with varying levels of linguistic proficiency, thus predefine challenges to EAP programs in Pakistan.

CONCLUSION

We have argued in this paper that the effects of Pakistani plurilingual repertoire can be observed in the hampered and perplexed language of explicit responses to texts (cf. instructional audio texts), responses which reflect the local linguistic landscape, including teaching resources that are bilingual and rely on translations. Negotiation of MOI thus becomes essential, regardless of the platform (social networks, print and digital media, etc.), to mediate a suitable mode of communication that is compatible to the local needs of the educational system, and all stakeholders. At this point in time, the aspirations of EAP learners, educators, and decision makers demonstrate this need in their positive attitudes to speech variation and linguistic tolerance in Pakistani plurilingual repertoire. Research suggests that for fuller participation of learners, EAP programs need to develop their meta-awareness of how language works (Canagarajah, 2009; Jiménez & Teague, 2009; Khubchandani, 2008; Lindholm-Leary, 2006; Meltzer & Hamann, 2005; Roessingh, 2004). The need for acceptance of plurilingual practices in EAP programs requires "a degree of planning, encouraging proficiency in the language of the classroom and in the languages of learners" (Khubchandani, 2008, p. 376). A holistic approach to education would recognize the presence of other languages, providing opportunities to take advantage of multilingualism and multilingual literacy (Cenoz & Gorter, 2011). Any decisions have to consider the growing plurilingual environment in local settings that keeps pace with globalization, modernization, and the socioeconomic demands of the people. The gradual absence of the national language, Urdu, in secondary schooling, and its nonexistence in professional education, weakens its presence in social discourse. We emphasize the recognition of local languages, and the plurilingual repertoire in Pakistani social settings, as well as academic settings, as not only a functional necessity; we believe recognition of the diversity of speakers' plurilingual repertoires would also lead to linguistic tolerance that would help in developing a sense of respect for social, cultural, and linguistic differences among professionals, participants, and all the stakeholders who contribute to the socio-academic discourse of Pakistan. It is necessary for the country's educational policy to recognise, and emphasize, the existence of plurilingual repertoire to cultivate a vision of respect for the linguistic rights of individuals and groups, of linguistic majorities and minorities, and of respect for freedom of their communication.

NOTES

[1] The Graeco-Latin square helped in sequencing the audios so that each student heard them in a different sequence,
where
E= English language
U=Urdu language
P=*Pakistani[1]*
and
n=narrative

e=expository
i=instructional

En	Ue	Pi
Ui	Pn	Ee
Pe	Ei	Un

REFERENCES

Annamalai, E. (2001). *Managing multilingualism in India: Political and linguistic manifestations.* New Delhi, India: Sage Publications.

Ashraf, H. (2008). The language of schooling and social capital in Pakistan. *NUML Research Magazine, 1*(1), 73-89.

Bhatia, T. K., & Ritchie, W. C. (2004). *The handbook of bilingualism.* Malden, MA: Blackwell.

Blommaert, J. (2010). *The sociolinguistics of globalization.* Cambridge, UK: Cambridge University Press.

Blommaert, J., & Verschueren, J. (1998). *Debating diversity: Analysing the discourse of tolerance.* London: Routledge.

Canagarajah, A. S. (2009). The plurilingual tradition and the English language in South Asia. *AILA Review, 22*(1), 5-22.

Canagarajah, A. S. (2011). Codemeshing in academic writing: Identifying teachable strategies of translanguaging. *The Modern Language Journal, 95*(3), 401-417.

Canagarajah, A. S. (2013). *Translingual practice: Global Englishes and cosmopolitan relations.* New York: Routledge.

Canagarajah, A. S., & Ashraf, H. (2013). Policy and practice on multilingual education in South Asia. *Annual Review of Applied Linguistics, 33*, 258-285.

Cenoz, J., & Gorter, D. (2011). A holistic approach to multilingual education: Introduction. *The Modern Language Journal, 95*(3), 339-343.

Coyle, D., Hood, P., & Marsh, D. (2010). *CLIL: Content and language integrated learning.* New York: Cambridge University Press.

García, O. (2009). *Bilingual education in the 21st century: A global perspective.* Malden, MA: Wiley-Blackwell.

García, O. (2011). From language garden to sustainable languaging: Bilingual education in a global world. *Perspective. A publication of the National Association for Bilingual Education, Nov/Dec*, 5-9.

Gillett, A. (2004). The ABC of ELA: EAP – English for academic purposes. *IATEFL Issues, 178*(11). http://www.uefap.com/articles/issues.htm

Hakim, L. (2010). *Analysis of marked and unmarked code choices by Pakistani bilingual students.* (Unpublished Master's dissertation), National University of Modern Languages, Islamabad, Pakistan.

Higher Education Commission Pakistan. (2009). English language teaching reforms project. Retrieved July 14, 2013, from http://www.hec.gov.pk/InsideHEC/Divisions/LearningInnovation/ELTR/Pages/Phase%20I.aspx

Jiménez, R. T., & Teague, B. L. (2009). Language, literacy, and content: Adolescent English language learners. In L. M. Morrow, R. Rueda, & D. Lapp (Eds.), *Handbook of research on literacy and diversity* (pp. 114-134). New York: The Guilford Press.

Khubchandani, L. (2008). Language policy and education in the Indian subcontinent. In S. May & N. Hornberger (Eds.), *Encyclopedia of language and education* (2nd ed., Vol. 1, pp. 369-381). New York: Springer.

Lewis, M. P. (Ed.). (2009). *Ethnologue: Languages of the world* (Sixteenth ed.). Dallas, TX: SIL International.

Lindholm-Leary, K., & Borsato, G. (2006). Academic achievement. In F. Genesee, K. Lindholm-Leary, W. M. Saunders & D. Christian (Eds.), *Educating English language learners: A synthesis of research evidence* (pp. 176–222). New York: Cambridge University Press.

Littlejohn, A. (2008). Digging deeper: Learners' dispositions and strategy use. In G. Cane (Ed.), *Strategies in language learning and teaching* (pp. 68-81). Singapore: SEAMEO Regional Language Centre.

Mansoor, S. (2004). The status and role of regional languages in higher education in Pakistan. *Journal of Multilingual and Multicultural Development, 25*(4), 333-353.

Mansoor, S. (2005). *Language planning in higher education: A case study of Pakistan.* Karachi, Pakistan: Oxford University Press.

Mansoor, S., Hussain, N., Sikandar, A., & Ahsa, N. M. (Eds.). (2009). *Emerging issues in TEFL: Challenges for South Asia.* Karachi, Pakistan: Oxford University Press.

Mecartty, F. H. (2001). The effects of modality, information type and language experience on recall by foreign language learners of Spanish. *Hispania, 84*(2), 265-278.

Meltzer, J., & Hamann, E. T. (2005). *Meeting the literacy development needs of adolescent English language learners through content area learning, part two: Focus on classroom teaching and learning strategies.* Faculty Publications: Department of Teaching, Learning and Teacher Education. http://digitalcommons.unl.edu/teachlcarnfacpub/53

Ministry of Education. (1959). *Sharif report of the commission on national education.* Islamabad, Pakistan.

Ministry of Education. (2009). *National education policy.* Islamabad, Pakistan.

Mohanty, A. K. (2010). Languages, inequality and marginalization: Implications of the double divide in Indian multilingualism. *International Journal of the Sociology of Language, 205*, 131-154.

Moyer, M. G., & Martin Rojo, L. (2007). Language, migration and citizenship: new challenges in the regulation of bilingualism. In M. Heller (Ed.), *Bilingualism: A social approach* (pp. 137-160). London: Palgrave MacMillan.

Pattanayak, D. P. (1984). Language policies in multilingual states. In A. Gonzalez (Ed.), *Panagani: Language planning, implementation and evaluation* (pp. 75-92). Manila, Philippines: Linguistic Society of the Philippines.

Rahman, T. (2001). English-teaching institutions in Pakistan. *Journal of Multilingual and Multicultural Development, 22*(3), 242-261.

Rahman, T. (2002). *Language, ideology and power: Language learning among the Muslims of Pakistan and North India.* Karachi, Pakistan: Oxford University Press.

Rahman, T. (2009). Language ideology, identity and the commodification of language in the call centers of Pakistan. *Language in Society, 38*(2), 233-258.

Rahman, T. (2011). *From Hindi to Urdu: A social and political history.* Karachi, Pakistan: Oxford University Press.

Roessingh, H. (2004). Effective high school ESL programs: A synthesis and meta-analysis. *Canadian Modern Language Review, 60*(5), 611-636.

Schleppegrell, M. J., & O'Hallaron, C. L. (2011). Teaching academic language in L2 secondary settings. *Annual Review of Applied Linguistics, 31*(1), 3-18.

Shamim, F. (2008). Trends, issues and challenges in English language education in Pakistan. *Asia Pacific Journal of Education, 28*(3), 235-249.

Shamim, F. (2011). English as the language for development in Pakistan: Issues, challenges and possible solutions. In H. Coleman (Ed.), *Dreams and realities: Developing countries and the English language* (pp. 291-310). London: British Council.

Silverstein, M. (1996). Monoglot 'standard' in America: Standardization and metaphors of linguistic hegemony. In D. Brenneis & R. Macaulay (Eds.), *The matrix of language: Contemporary linguistic anthropology* (pp. 284-306). Boulder, CO: Westview Press.

Slimani, A. (2001). Evaluation of classroom interaction. In C. Candlin & N. Mercer (Eds.), *English language teaching in its social context: A reader* (pp. 287-305). London: Routledge.

Zulfiqar, I. (2012). *The effects of the interaction between monomodal and multimodal text on language performance in Pakistani ESL context: A longitudinal case study.* Unpublished doctoral dissertation, National University of Modern Languages, Islamabad, Pakistan.

Hina Ashraf
Department of Humanities
Faculty of Social Sciences
Air University, Islamabad, Pakistan

Luqman Hakim
Faculty of Advanced Integrated Studies & Research
National University of Modern Languages
Islambad, Pakistan

Irum Zulfiqar
Department of Humanities
Faculty of Social Sciences
Air University, Islamabad, Pakistan

MADHAV KAFLE

4. EAP IN NEPAL

Practitioner Perspectives on Multilingual Pedagogy

INTRODUCTION

For centuries before the arrival of Europeans, the language ecology in South Asia was multilingual (see Canagarajah & Liyanage, 2012; Pollock, 2006). The geopolitical situation of Nepal and its long sociocultural ties with India played a key role in the introduction of English education, and, even today, ecological factors contribute greatly to Nepalese English for Academic Purposes (EAP). Following colonization, multilingualism was labelled deficient and in the name of making pedagogies scientific, norms of the monolingual colonizer were implemented in education of a local elite needed to maintain the colony. Slowly, local knowledge was trivialized, labelled unscientific, backward, and invalid. English became a key aspect of divisions in Nepal between the elites and the masses that have been maintained intact in the post-colonial era (see Ramanathan, 2005a).

As availability of English education grew during early 20th century, Indian universities extended their services to Nepal and shared their expertise in teaching English using the grammar translation method with textbooks imported from India and classics of Western literature (Uprety, 1996). More recently, the educational use of English has not only contributed to maintenance of socioeconomic divisions, but has also provided access to broader areas of knowledge. Even though English is not yet officially a second language, it is used extensively, both in and outside academia, and has made technical and scientific knowledge of many fields accessible. English has become cultural capital (Bourdieu, 1991) sought after by both literate and non-literate Nepalese (see Giri, 2010; Uprety, 1996), and there has been a mushrooming of private schools, colleges, and media hubs devoted to its study and use. The Nepalese government has recently made English-language teaching mandatory in schools from Grade One (Government of Nepal Ministry of Education, 2009), indicative of the growing significance of the role of English in the education of the Nepalese population. With increasing globalization, higher education is being internationalized and research is flourishing in various themes. However, despite a growing body of international research on socially sensitive EAP pedagogies, teachers' perceptions of EAP pedagogy in periphery countries such as Nepal have been given scant attention.

I. Liyanage & T. Walker (eds.), English for Academic Purposes (EAP) in Asia, 51–64.

EAP in Nepal

EAP is one of the murkiest terms in English Language Teaching (ELT) and can refer to a diverse set of practices (Carkin, 2005; Hamp-Lyons, 2011). In Nepal, a multilingual country with at least 121 languages (Lewis, Simons, & Fennig, 2013), EAP can be broadly described using two situations identified by Carkin (2005): EAP in multilingual settings where English is used as the language of instruction throughout the education system; and EAP used in teaching specialty subjects such as medicine, technology, engineering, and science, as texts in languages other than English can be scarce in those fields. Although English is used as the default medium of instruction (MOI) in many fields in higher education in Nepal, we need to understand the nature of English use in these contexts as this might be quite different from the way English is used in so-called norm-providing countries. Even though the Nepal English Language Teachers' Association (NELTA) Journal, which publishes scholarship about English teaching in Nepal, was established in 1996, when browsing through its pages it becomes evident that there are not many articles that address generally the problems of EAP (see, however, Mishra, 1999). It is only recently that we can see discussions about specific challenges involved in EAP in NELTA Yahoo group discussions and in *"Nelta Choutari,"* a blog magazine run by Nepalese ELT teachers. Still, these online discussions cannot be generalized to the mass of teachers, even within Nepal, who might not have easy access to computers and the internet. Discussing how to match local needs and global demands might sound like a far cry in such a scenario. Recently, however, the need to strive for local scholarship has been voiced by a number of Nepalese ELT professionals (e.g. B. K. Sharma, 2013; S. Sharma, 2013), an encouraging sign that such discussions are timely.

Although there is a relative dearth of literature regarding Nepalese EAP practices, the existing literature identifies several challenges faced in EAP classrooms in Nepal: large classes and lack of adequate teaching resources (Giri, 2010); disconnect between policy and practice (Kafle, 2013a); inadequacy of professional development (Gautam, 1998); and neglect of local needs (Kafle, 2013b; S. Sharma, 2013). Other problems include determination of the variety of English to be taught, selection of methodologies that best suit Nepalese contexts (Giri, 2010), and the often enormous gaps between the proficiency of learners coming from private schools and those from public or government schools. Thus, while scholars in developed countries might be busy debating the best model of teaching academic language and literacy, for many teachers in Nepal problems are centred on more fundamental issues. One of the major challenges has been the nature of knowledge construction in so-called periphery countries like Nepal, where anything Western seems to be accepted as of superior quality (see B. K. Sharma, 2013). Although this is not a problem restricted to language teaching per se, and can apply to many other disciplines, it is a problem far too important to be ignored. This chapter explores major challenges faced by EAP professionals in Nepal: the development of socially sensitive pedagogies, and negotiation of tensions that arise in this process.

THE STUDY

To study those challenges of EAP professionals in Nepal, an online qualitative survey was disseminated to 16 English teachers through the NELTA Yahoo group, emails, and social networks. The survey included general questions about teachers' background information and several focus questions asking teachers to describe various aspects of their experiences of teaching EAP in Nepal and their perceptions of the role and future of EAP. The survey focus questions were:

- What problems have you experienced so far regarding teaching English in Nepal? How have you overcome them?
- How do you often negotiate tensions (if any) between Western ELT practices and local circumstances?
- What prospects do you see for teaching English for Academic Purposes in Nepal?
- With the increasing trend of internationalization of higher education worldwide, in what ways can Nepal better prepare itself in terms of teaching English for Academic Purposes?

Among the 14 participants were seven university professors, four higher secondary teachers, one secondary teacher, one primary teacher, and one part-time teacher. Initial letters of participants' names are used to identify the sources of data excerpts in the findings, below. The participant responses were compiled in a single file and coded thematically on four major areas: problems, tensions, prospects, and internationalization. Since data were generated through an online survey, the discussions below might not represent opinions of teachers in more remote regions of the country where access to computers and the internet is difficult. As EAP was not defined in the survey, participants' responses revealed diverse understandings of EAP within the broader field of English-language teaching. Nevertheless, teachers' perceptions of EAP presented in what follows assist in understanding the current status of EAP practices in Nepal, and provide some guidance for the conduct of future research, as well as insights for consideration in any adjustments of current pedagogical practices.

FINDINGS AND DISCUSSION

Teachers in Nepal experience significant problems related to elementary issues such as class sizes, teaching materials and resources, technology, and even infrastructure. Concerns that the quality of teaching and learning is severely affected by large classes with which teachers are constantly confronted are widespread. In the universities, classes are massively large; each class can comprise more than 200 with insufficient seating to accommodate them. RL (Lines 100-102), who teaches at the university level in Kathmandu, voices these concerns: "*I have to teach as many as some 150 students in a group. So, I cannot provide them with opportunities to learn. Neither can we scaffold them giving feedbacks in their written works.*" At high school level, where, to graduate, students have to pass a national exam called School Leaving Certificate, teachers are facing similar constraints on effective teaching and learning, and, the failure rate in English is cripplingly high (Giri, 2011). The challenges of achieving quality teaching and learning in large classes are compounded by the paucity of time allocated to the study of English in the curriculum, a factor some teachers identified as critical to learner success as "*only 45 minutes class of English is not sufficient for developing English on the part of students*" (RM: Lines 63-64). High school teacher AM (Lines 487-490) summed up the situation thus: "*there are more than 50 learners in a single class. Correction of assignment is problematic. The learners do not get enough time to practice language and to get feedback on their errors.*" Overall, the participants agreed with the judgement of RM that "*in the context of Nepalese EFL setting, especially in remote public schools in Nepal, the conditions and outcomes are bitter*" (RM: Lines 62-63); many institutions have limited facilities and are unable to provide environments conducive to learning in which learners have access to good libraries and the internet, creating a cycle of under-resourcing and under-performance.

Teaching and learning is further complicated due to the enormous gap between the proficiency of learners coming from private schools and those from public or government schools. As PL (Lines 269-270) observes, "*students coming from private schools are better at coping with English than the students coming from community schools.*" Many students have completed their schooling in rural villages and, for most, unless they are taught English in Nepali language:

> ... they cannot understand. Majority of the students in Nepal are from rural parts and they are very poor in English. Most of them can neither write nor produce good sentences in English for communicative purposes. As a result, they pass all the subjects except English. (YP: Lines 568-570)

Similarly, AC (Lines 442-443), a higher secondary level teacher, faces "*different kinds of problems in teaching English because it is teaching [taught] as a secondary language, so the average level of students cannot understand it without translating into Nepali.*" These teachers raise a crucial issue as, despite these unbridgeable variations in proficiency, all students face difficult exams at the end of the semester.

For teachers themselves, shortcomings in English proficiency and inadequate training are significant problems that impact on practitioners' capacities to develop pedagogies that respond to global demands given local needs. RG (Lines 14-17), a teacher trainer and university lecturer, is in no doubt that "*English language proficiency of the teachers is a major problem. ... In order to overcome them, I have been involved in the teacher training activities both at the university level and at the professional level.*" We need to understand that by training activities, RG means encouraging teachers to follow Western methods and approaches to language teaching and learning, such as the communicative approach. Even with training, teachers might not be able to address the problems in their classes. Problems are created cumulatively because, in the first instance, teachers who lack training are expected to use Western teaching materials; when trained, teachers often find Western teaching methods do not lend to the local contexts. As

54

mentioned on its website, NELTA is working hard to train teachers because "departure from structural teaching to communicative teaching demanded massive teacher training and orientation, which the government could not do alone" (Nepal English Language Teachers' Association (NELTA), n.d). Nevertheless, without theorizing local pedagogical practices, connecting Western-sourced teaching materials and resources to local contexts is highly challenging for teachers of EAP.

Mode of assessment is another area where teachers have to negotiate in their own ways. As the testing system is examination oriented, rather than communicative, it is natural for learners to want to "*get more score or pass the exam rather than learning language itself*" (AM: Line 126). Extensive use of simplified versions of original texts and "*mugging up*" (PC) is common. For SG, a former ELT practitioner from Nepal:

> ... the biggest problem of teaching English in Nepal is that it is limited to teaching for the exams, covering the course (which is nothing but the prescribed textbook), and repeating the same thing year after year. There is no incentive whatsoever for teaching differently, for challenging and inspiring students toward more engaging/fruitful learning. (SG: Lines 325-330)

In this scenario, in which the approach is centred on a set of standards to be achieved, teaching and learning tends to concentrate on English for testing purposes, rather than on English for academic purposes.

The remainder of this section highlights tensions created by the disconnect of local and global norms and practices as seen in top-down imposition of the curriculum and dismissal of hybrid practices. Despite viewing data from a decidedly binary perspective the goal is not to reify a dichotomy between local and global constituents. Rather, it is the opposite: The goal is to show how working on a binary paradigm can restrict us, and thus to highlight the need for negotiation of multiple norms.

One of the questions in the survey focussed on the perceptions of the teachers about possible tensions they have experienced between Western and local discourses of English, and ELT, and their strategies of dealing with it. Many teachers stressed that they perceive multiple tensions around various teaching components, including textbooks, teaching methodologies, and language-in-education policies. For instance, monolingual policy rules out the possibility of using students' prior linguistic experience. Even though teachers use hybrid practices in their classes, they often do not get credit for trying to better connect the curriculum to the students. Similarly, the use of non-local textbooks creates problems because often the characters and place names used in the books are too removed from local realities (PS).

Since universities in Nepal use a fixed set of textbooks recommended by curriculum committees, individual instructors cannot prescribe books for the courses they teach. They can suggest additional resources, however, as YP: Line 187 opines, "*it is a great challenge to implement the 'global' textbooks written or prepared by the Western writers who, I don't think, even have any slightest idea about our context."* Some prescribed books have ideas, concepts, and learning activities stretched far away from the local reality. For example, the texts ask teachers:

> ... to engage our students in different group work and pair work activities but the problem is we never learnt to do so. We have different culture so some of the common ideas written in those books are not digestible for our students. (WU: Lines 411-414)

Even when teaching materials are published locally, content is not adapted to local realities. The content of textbooks "has little to do with the lives of students outside of the need to take and pass the exams; it has little to do with the society and material reality of their world" (SG: Lines 333-335). Textbooks *"adopted directly from the Western ambience are not suitable to Nepalese students as they are far removed from the social, psychological, economic and educational realities"* (PL: Lines 274-276). Teachers negotiate the challenges these course-books and materials present in a variety of ways. PL, for example, says that he is able to use his knowledge of the Western world to facilitate teaching, but not all teachers are well versed in knowledge of the Western world. Before beginning the courses he teaches, YP tells the students that course-books are just the media and not the means, and tries to raise critical awareness by encouraging students to question issues raised in course-books from the perspective of the local teaching context. According to him, what matters most for teachers is *"how we garner insights from these global textbooks to explore our own teaching learning situation,"* but the process of reaping insights from the texts disconnected from the Nepalese context is not easy.

On a similar note, teachers find the educational policy mandating the monolingual use of English in classrooms in a multilingual country like Nepal *"absurd"* (RL: Line 129). Some, such as RL, resist the monolingual English imperative:

> ... communicative language teaching or task-based language teaching rarely suggests us to use mother tongue in the language classroom. However, in reality, I translate the texts in Nepali, which is the mother tongue of almost all the students of my campus. (RL: Lines 125-128)

Similarly, another teacher, KB, characterizes the current overemphasis on English in the sense that English is thriving at the cost of Nepali, as well as many other indigenous languages. KB believes that language is closely connected with identity and culture; however, teachers are asked to follow teaching methodologies imported from the West (see Government of Nepal Ministry of Education, 2009).Since Western teaching methodologies are often not applicable to local Nepalese contexts, teachers have the task of negotiating practices locally:

> Recent researches [sic] on SLA focus on the methods like Task Based Language Learning, and Communicative Language Teaching. However, in our EFL context the need to use language in real life is minimal. The learners

are less [familiar] with such methods. They are habitual with teacher-centred methods. I use range of methods from teacher centred to learner centred and want to be eclectic while selecting methods rather than sticking with some particular methods. (AM: Lines 490-495)

Simply adopting communicative language teaching practices creates more problems than it solves for teachers and learners, as seen in many other settings (see Hu, 2005; Nishino & Watanabe, 2008; Nunan, 2003; Zappa-Hollman, 2007).

Top-down imposition of curriculum means designing of curriculum befitting to the local context is almost impossible in the Nepalese context. Almost all universities in Nepal, and their branch campuses, operate on a centralized curriculum that is imposed without necessarily establishing any connection with local needs and proficiencies of students. Not only the goals and objectives of courses, but also the teaching materials, are defined beforehand by subject committees, and teachers across the nation are supposed to follow the same syllabi using the same materials despite any variations in setting and student population. It might be easier from the administrative perspective, but, as AB highlights, top-down polices create problems:

... problems are many, ranging from situational and institutional constraints to designing and implementation of curriculum. Of them, the gap between the objectives and the spirit of the curriculum and the level as well as expectations of students is the most striking one. So far, [in] the course I teach, the course objectives, contents, methodology suggested do not address the pedagogical constraints imposed by the classroom realities such as number of students, level of students, their educational backgrounds. (AB: Lines 154-160)

Findings of this study suggest this disconnect between learners' local realities and the imposed curriculum is found throughout the nation, and indeed mirrors a similar disconnect between policy and practice in many countries such as India, South Africa, Tanzania, Kenya, and Malaysia (Lin & Martin, 2005). The "*most crucial*" problem facing EAP teachers is that "*ELT in Nepal is top-down. Teachers are not provided any significant role to play in all aspects*" (NH, Lines 296-297). Despite that, while teachers are trying to follow prescribed methodologies, many devise their own ways of combating the disengagement of learners.

Rather than impose conceptions and academic practices embedded in Western teaching methods and approaches in sociocultural and institutional settings in Nepal (see Hyland, 2006), teachers understand the need to explore what kinds of variations emerge across contexts and the need to strive for the development of local pedagogies. However, the major challenge remains defining locally informed and situated practices; a huge question for teachers, and EAP in Nepal, is how to imagine multilingual schools (García, Skutnabb-Kangas, & Torres-Guzmán, 2006). Despite the problems and challenges outlined above, all the study participants agree, with some degree of variation, that EAP is essential in Nepal. However, equally significantly, findings reveal that this agreement is tempered by some uncertainty about what constitutes EAP. Some teachers equate the current teaching practice of use of English for educational purposes with EAP. Others think that EAP is a new discipline for the Nepalese context, and teachers have yet to specialize in it. Some would even say EAP does not exist in Nepal. RG, a past president of NELTA and a highly experienced trainer of teachers who has completed courses in American universities, is cognizant of how the term EAP is often used in the ELT profession, and believes EAP is:

> ... very much needed in Nepal. We did not have a course of this kind in our university system in the past. Now, I have included EAP course in the newly established universities. I am sure, the new course will give us the opportunity to see how it goes in Nepal. (RG: Lines 24-27)

The vernacular divide that has been one of the problems challenging teachers in their practice is closing, as most community schools in Nepal shift their MOI from Nepali to English "*to attract students, compete with private English-medium schools and provide quality education. English has been the key to success in life in Nepalese society*" (YP). According to RL, there is a new audience for English in Nepal and the need for EAP is urgent, a view indicative of the higher prospect of EAP if knowledge is to be democratized:

> I think there are a lot of prospects of academic English in Nepal. Let me list them. Journalism, science and technology, business and commerce are to list but very few. In the present scenario, the media are booming up in Nepal. So are the audience who need the news, views, and other stuffs in English. So, many students want to learn the kind of English that is used for writing feature stories, anchoring, news reporting, writing news in an English daily, etc. Tourism. Tourist guide training centres in Nepal teach English to their trainees the kind of English they are likely to encounter when they become tourist guides. (RL: Lines 129-137)

Likewise, AB draws attention to the role of EAP in the issue of knowledge capital, in moving from the position of knowledge consumer to knowledge producer:

> ... teaching EAP is the demand of our time and it is good that EAP is one of the most burgeoning areas of ELT in Nepal. Current English courses prescribed for the Bachelor in Education can be a case in point. Recently we ELT practitioners in Nepal have realized the fact that teaching English for communication is important but not sufficient to help our students survive in the present world that values knowledge capital. This calls for skills of acquiring (through reading) and producing (through writing) information/knowledge. Our focus on EAP courses will lead us to producer of knowledge from that of mere consumers. (AB: Lines 173-181)

Although, on the one hand, participants express optimistic prospects for the role of EAP, on the other, what also emerges from the data are troubling indications that EAP teachers experience personal conflict about the roles they are playing in shifts in the linguistic landscape of Nepal. They observe that, although "*English is an international language, so in the academic arena, the use of English has been increasing day by day*" (RM: Lines 60-61), "*there is not any research to support teaching of English from Grade 1. It is still an elitist practice*" (NH: Lines 309-310). The prospects for teachers themselves at a professional level clearly need careful consideration when they feel their vocation is based on a cultural artefact that "*has been designed, developed and delivered as a dominating language*" (KB: Lines 214-215), and that English is a seductive brand that everyone is willing to buy:

> English is in the end nothing but a brand name for a needless product that most people are bound to buy because it is a cultural capital without which it is getting harder and harder to be successful in Nepal. It is very unfortunate. (SG: Lines 356-359)

In such a context, how EAP teachers should proceed and be prepared are crucial questions. As professionals they are uniquely placed to facilitate increased use of English as a global language in Nepal, a phenomenon which appears irresistible, and to simultaneously adopt a resistant stance in response to vital local needs and interests.

DISCUSSION

The teachers involved in this study raised many questions about the current state of EAP in Nepal, and its future, as an effective means of preparing learners for participation in a globalized world. The disconnect experienced by teachers between policies and practices can only be solved with reconfigurations of numerous issues. In the words of participant AB, both government and private sectors have overemphasized English in the name of modern pedagogies and quality improvement. Such overemphasis carries a price:

> The overemphasis on the English-only medium has been at the cost of our national languages and quality of learning. My observation is that in the private schools, students have problems in understanding the basic concepts in the content areas like Social Studies and Science not because the topic itself is so difficult but primarily because the teacher fails to make them understand in English. Now the options open to us are a) We either teach English to these non-English teachers or b) we adopt the Nepali language as a medium of instruction. (AB: Lines 194-201)

As is customary in many Asian countries, English is often perceived as a vehicle for development and equated with success (see Sung & Pederson, 2012). By consciously or unconsciously promoting Standard English and maintaining the status quo, ELT professionals not only literally fail students from government schools, we also fail to support students from private schools to realize their full potentials. The argument here is not that English is not important, but simply that we should be reflective of the language practices in Nepalese society, as participants of this study urge. While the role of English as a killer language is still

KAFLE

hotly debated (see Nettle & Romaine, 2000; Saxena & Omoniyi, 2010), complete rejection of English would not make sense either. Perhaps developing countries like Nepal might look to the example of the European Union where language learning and linguistic diversity is promoted in the name of employability, mobility, and the demands of a knowledge-based economy.

As SG observes, English in Nepal has been taught in a vacuum and used as an elite language. Although not all the teachers would agree, SG (Lines 368-370) argues "*English should be just a subject and not a medium of instruction at all levels and for all subjects. The concept and practice of English for academic purposes should be introduced.*" He goes on to say that university education should be delivered in English only in appropriate subjects. English teachers should not only focus on examinations success, but also teach to enable students to use the language beyond the classroom. Internationalization of education based on the use of English spreading the dominance of Western paradigms will continue exacerbating loss of local knowledge and diversity of linguistic and academic practices. Critical EAP practitioners argue that *needs analysis* of the learners should also constitute *rights analysis* (Benesch, 2001) and transcend the pragmatic orientation of EAP to strike a balance between local and global pedagogies (see e.g. edited volumes by Alsagoff, McKay, Hu, & Renandya, 2012; Rubdy & Saraceni, 2006; Sharifian, 2009). To transcend the dichotomy between local and global and to validate the hybridity of linguistic practices we can also draw upon trans-theories (Pennycook, 2007) or transidiomatic practices (Jacquemet, 2005), which recognize that teaching language cannot be a neutral enterprise, but is often laced with the political, economic, social, and cultural aspects.

In the global knowledge economy, knowledge should flow bilaterally, if not multilaterally. Training teachers to understand the richness of local linguistic resources, and to utilize these in such a way that all parties benefit, is crucial if we are to respectably take part in the global economy. As RG (Lines 27-30) says, Nepal can best prepare itself by "*exposing our students to the global education and by exposing our indigenous knowledge to the global audience. So far the former is the case. Our approach now should give equal emphasis for the later one.*" Teachers should also be trained to navigate the demands of local and global discourses in their everyday classrooms, to build upon their own experiences (see Liyanage, 2010, for Sri Lankan context) in development of local pedagogies: "*in contrast to top-to-bottom, bottom-to-top approach should be followed while preparing the curriculum for teaching English for academic purposes*" (YP: Lines 594-596).

Now the question is: Can we achieve that? Fortunately, we have now a repository of local pedagogies across the globe. de Souza (2005) provides an example from Kashinawa writing, which uses complex multimodal features; Ramanathan (2005b) highlights the role of choral repetition in India; Nishino and Watanabe (2008) emphasize the importance of grammar translation in Japan; Chen, Warden, and Chang (2005) show how examination-oriented motivation can work in better terms in Taiwan (see Bannink, 2010; Canagarajah, 2012).We can build on these examples and conduct research to fulfil the gap in Nepalese ELT/EAP.

We can also draw forth from excellent findings from the English as lingua franca (ELF) research, which has assisted us in unpacking various foci, for example, phonology (Jenkins, 2000), lexicon and grammar (Seidlhofer, 2009), and pragmatics (House, 2009). Firth (2009) has established that we cannot label non-native speakers deficient any more. To accomplish such goal(s), what Canagarajah (2013) calls translingual pedagogy, or others call translanguaging pedagogy (see Creese & Blackledge, 2011; García, 2009), can be useful. Translingual approaches build on hybrid semiotic practices, destabilize the concept of the monolithic standard, and shift goals of teaching from mastery of target norms to effective negotiation of divergent communicative practices. Many other related concepts such as code-meshing (Canagarajah, 2006; Young, 2004), continua of biliteracy (Hornberger, 2003), and metrolingualism (Pennycook, 2010) are used to refer to the dynamic language-mixing practices of multilinguals. With these practices, we can counter the monolingual, ideologically driven (Blackledge, 2000) policy imposed on multilingual Nepal. In that future, teaching a language would not mean making learners conform to the *homogeneous norms* of some particular brand of English, but making them aware of the semiotic practices they would need in various situations. Therefore, as suggested in this paper, we need to give credence to what students and teachers frequently do in their classrooms and let them decide how they can best connect their local needs (see Bhattarai, 1999) and global demands.

CONCLUSION

As ELT professionals in this study suggest, neither a wholesale adoption of global pedagogy nor a clinging to a narrow sense of localness can do justice to widening EAP pedagogy. Although there might be some challenges in theorizing the local EAP pedagogy in Nepalese and similar other contexts, we need to first start reflecting on our own actual set of practices, which create knowledge and assist in developing locally tuned pedagogies. We need to strive to see that what we have been doing so far is not mimicry of Western methodologies but a collective enterprise that both is shaped by, and shapes, our process of knowledge production. We need to hark back to our multilingual past and revive local knowledge from its invalidated state and treat it as compatible with other types of knowledge. I am not saying that we should thwart the use of global methods. In fact, in a post-neoliberal world we would much need to learn the spirit of the clichéd phrase *think globally, act locally*.

It is often assumed that there is not much exposure to English language in Nepal outside academia. However, much depends on what we mean by *English* and *language*. Even the remotest village of Nepal is now connected with some kind of technology, and transnational contacts are not hard to imagine. In such a situation, people will have different degrees of English competence and will utilize multimodal and multilingual practices to take part in global flows of ideas and commodities. Once we recognize and start to value such hybrid practices in academic settings as well, then we will also see the ramifications they might have on other complementary parts of pedagogy. This means not only redesigning the curriculum, and rethinking teaching methodologies and assessment techniques from ground up, but also reimagining expertise and success.

If we can treat global knowledge as analogous to local knowledge, as the paradigm which, for socio-historical reasons, has now become dominant (Canagarajah, 2005), we can begin to see the possibilities in current local pedagogies. In that perspective, the global does not have to be necessarily superior, but we need research at the local level to evaluate indigenous methodologies. One of the problems of developing and researching local knowledge in Nepal is the under-theorized nature of the local knowledge. Meanwhile, local knowledge is not a static body of wisdom to be discovered; it is in constant play with other discourses, absorbing the global as the global is absorbing the local. It is interesting to note that people are only starting to see the importance of hybrid linguistic practices. In late modernity, the assumption of the dominant pedagogy that linguistic diversity in classrooms is a problem is being challenged as texts become more multivocal. In such a context, to meet demands of the knowledge economy, Nepalese EAP practitioners should be mindful of not only global demands but also their students' local needs.

REFERENCES

Alsagoff, L., McKay, S. L., Hu, G., & Renandya, W. A. (Eds.). (2012). *Principles and practices for teaching English as an international language.* New York: Routledge.

Bannink, A. (2010). West meets East: On the necessity of local pedagogies. *Journal of Intercultural Communication, 24.* Retrieved from http://www.immi.se/intercultural/ website: http://www.immi.se/intercultural/nr24/bannink.htm

Benesch, S. (2001). *Critical English for academic purposes: Theory, politics and practice.* London: Lawrence Erlbaum.

Bhattarai, G. R. (1999). A proposal for resituating translation in our curriculum. *Journal of NELTA, 4*(2), 13-15.

Blackledge, A. (2000). Monolingual ideologies in multilingual states: Language, hegemony and social justice in Western liberal democracies. *Sociolinguistic Studies, 1*(2), 25-45.

Bourdieu, P. (1991). *Language and symbolic power.* Cambridge, UK: Polity.

Canagarajah, A. S. (2005). *Reclaiming the local in language policy and practice.* Mahwah, NJ: Lawrence Erlbaum.

Canagarajah, A. S. (2006). The place of World Englishes in composition: Pluralization continued. *College Composition and Communication, 57*(2), 586-619.

Canagarajah, A. S. (2012). Teacher development in a global profession: An autoethnography. *TESOL Quarterly, 46*(2), 258-279.

Canagarajah, A. S. (Ed.). (2013). *Literacy as translingual practice: Between communities and classrooms.* London: Routledge.

Canagarajah, A. S., & Liyanage, I. (2012). Lessons from pre-colonial multilingualism. In M. Martin-Jones, A. Blackledge, & A. Creese (Eds.), *The Routledge handbook of multilingualism* (pp. 49-65). London: Routledge.

Carkin, S. (2005). English for academic purposes. In E. Hinkel (Ed.), *Handbook of research in second language teaching and learning* (Vol. I, pp. 85-98). Mahwah, NJ: Lawrence Erlbaum.

Chen, J. F., Warden, C. A., & Chang, H.-t. (2005). Motivators that do not motivate: The case of Chinese EFL learners and the influence of culture on motivation. *TESOL Quarterly, 39*(4), 609-633.

Creese, A., & Blackledge, A. (2011). Separate and flexible bilingualism in complementary schools: Multiple language practices in interrelationship. *Journal of Pragmatics, 43*(5), 1196-1208.

de Souza, L. M. (2005). The ecology of writing among the Kashinama: Indigenous multimodality in Brazil. In A. S. Canagarajah (Ed.), *Reclaiming the local in language policy and practice* (pp. 73-95). Mahwah, NJ: Lawrence Erlbaum.

Firth, A. (2009). Doing not being a foreign language learner: English as a lingua franca in the workplace and (some) implications for SLA. *International Review of Applied Linguistics in Language Teaching, 47*(1), 127-156.

García, O. (2009). *Bilingual education in the 21st century: A global perspective.* Malden, MA: Wiley-Blackwell.

García, O., Skutnabb-Kangas, T., & Torres-Guzmán, M. E. (2006). *Imagining multilingual schools: Languages in education and glocalization.* Bristol, UK: Multilingual Matters.

Gautam, G. R. (1998). Professional development in ELT. *Journal of NELTA, 3*(1-2), 98-104.

Giri, R. A. (2010). English language teachers' resource centre: A model for developing contexts. *Journal of NELTA, 15*(1-2), 64-76.

Giri, R. A. (2011). Examination as an agent of educational reform: Re-iterating some issues of debate. Retrieved from http://neltachoutari.wordpress.com/2011/05/01/1645/

Government of Nepal Ministry of Education. (2009). *School sector reform plan 2009-2015.* Retrieved from http://www.moe.gov.np/attachments/article/32/SSRP%20English.pdf.

Hamp-Lyons, L. (2011). English for academic purposes. In E. Hinkel (Ed.), *Handbook of research in second language teaching and learning* (Vol. 2, pp. 89-105). New York: Routledge.

Hornberger, N. H. (2003). *Continua of biliteracy: An ecological framework for educational policy, research, and practice in multilingual settings* (Vol. 41). Bristol, UK: Multilingual Matters.

House, J. (2009). Introduction: The pragmatics of English as a lingua franca. *Intercultural Pragmatics, 6*(2), 141-145.

Hu, G. (2005). Contextual influences on instructional practices: A Chinese case for an ecological approach to ELT. *TESOL Quarterly, 39*(4), 635-660.

Hyland, K. (2006). *English for academic purposes: An advanced resource book.* New York: Routledge.

Jacquemet, M. (2005). Transidiomatic practices: Language and power in the age of globalization. *Language & Communication, 25*(3), 257-277.

Jenkins, J. (2000). *The phonology of English as an international language.* Oxford, UK: Oxford University Press.

Kafle, M. (2013a). Editorial, July 2013: Local pedagogies in multilingual settings. Retrieved from http://neltachoutari.wordpress.com/2013/07/01/local-pedagogies-in-multilingual-settings/

Kafle, M. (2013b). Monolingual practices in multilingual states: Implications for language teaching. Retrieved from http://neltachoutari.wordpress.com/2013/03/01/monolingual-policies-in-multilingual-states-implications-for-language-teaching/

Lewis, M. P., Simons, G. F., & Fennig, C. D. (Eds.). (2013). *Nepal* (Seventeenth ed.). Dallas, TX: SIL International.

Lin, A. M., & Martin, P. W. (2005). *Decolonisation, globalisation: Language-in-education policy and practice* (Vol. 3). Clevedon, UK: Multilingual Matters Ltd.

Liyanage, I. (2010). Globalisation: Medium-of-instruction policy, indigenous educational systems and ELT in Sri Lanka. In V. Vaish (Ed.), *Globalization of language and culture in Asia* (pp. 209-232). London: Continuum.

Mishra, C. (1999). Role of the teacher in the EFL/ESL classroom. *Journal of NELTA, 4*(2), 28-33.

Nepal English Language Teachers' Association (NELTA). (n.d). Emergence of NELTA. Retrieved July 5, 2013, from http://www.nelta.org.np/about/emergence_of_nelta.html

Nettle, D., & Romaine, S. (2000). *Vanishing voices: The extinction of the world's languages.* Oxford, UK: Oxford University Press.

Nishino, T., & Watanabe, M. (2008). Communication-oriented policies versus classroom realities in Japan. *TESOL Quarterly, 42*(1), 133-138.

63

Nunan, D. (2003). The impact of English as a global language on educational policies and practices in the Asia-Pacific region. *TESOL Quarterly, 37*(4), 589-613.

Pennycook, A. (2007). *Global Englishes and transcultural flows.* New York: Routledge.

Pennycook, A. (2010). *Language as a local practice.* New York: Routledge.

Pollock, S. (2006). *The language of the gods in the world of men: Sanskrit, culture, and power in premodern India.* Berkeley, CA: University of California Press.

Ramanathan, V. (2005a). *The English-vernacular divide: Postcolonial language politics and practice.* Bristol, UK: Multilingual Matters.

Ramanathan, V. (2005b). Seepages, contact zones, and amalgam: Internationalizing TESOL. *TESOL Quarterly, 39*(1), 119-123.

Rubdy, R., & Saraceni, M. (Eds.). (2006). *English in the world: Global rules, global roles.* New York: Continuum.

Saxena, M., & Omoniyi, T. (Eds.). (2010). *Contending with globalization in world Englishes.* Bristol, UK: Multilingual Matters.

Seidlhofer, B. (2009). Common ground and different realities: World Englishes and English as a lingua franca. *World Englishes, 28*(2), 236-245.

Sharifian, F. (Ed.). (2009). *English as an international language: Perspectives and pedagogical issues.* Bristol, UK: Multilingual Matters.

Sharma, B. K. (2013). Hinduism and TESOL: Learning, teaching and student-teacher relationships revisited. *Language and Linguistics Compass, 7*(2), 79-90.

Sharma, S. (2013). SLC, ELT, and our place in the big picture. Retrieved from http://neltachoutari.wordpress.com/2013/07/01/slc-elt-and-our-place-in-the-big-picture/

Sung, K., & Pederson, R. (2012). Critical practices in ELT as a project of possibilities or a banal discourse. In K. Sung & R. Pederson (Eds.), *Critical ELT practices in Asia* (pp. 153-169). Boston, MA: Sense Publishers.

Uprety, N. (1996). English education in Nepal. *Journal of NELTA, 1*(2), 23-27.

Young, V. A. (2004). Your average nigga. *College Composition and Communication, 55*(4), 693-715.

Zappa-Hollman, S. (2007). EFL in Argentina's schools: Teachers' perspectives on policy changes and instruction. *TESOL Quarterly, 41*(3), 618-625.

Madhav Kafle
Pennsylvania State University
USA

MAYA GUNAWARDENA & ELENI PETRAKI

5. CRITICAL THINKING SKILLS IN THE EAP CLASSROOM

Negotiating Tensions in the Sri Lankan Context

INTRODUCTION

The role of critical thinking has been at the heart of a controversial debate in English for Academic Purposes (EAP) circles, dividing Western and non-Western, particularly Asian, education. Some researchers consider critical thinking as the preserve and ideal of Western education (Durkin, 2008; Egege & Kutieleh, 2004; Walker & Finney, 1999) and a significant gap in Asian students' learning. This reified view, based on research conducted with students who study in Western universities, regards lack of critical thinking as a deficit (Egege & Kutieleh, 2004). In response to these claims, Kumaravadivelu (2003) suggests that such views put Asian students into stereotypical cultural baskets because students' performances can be influenced by limited English-language skills and cultural differences. What is missing in this debate is research that examines critical thinking practices of students in Asian contexts.

Critical thinking is often discussed as a "non overt and slippery" (Dwight Atkinson, 1997, p. 75) concept. It has been defined as "reasonable reflective thinking" (Ennis, 1989, p. 10) or a set of cognitive skills, such as conceptualizing, applying, analyzing, synthesizing, and/or evaluating information by reasoning or communication (Walker & Finney, 1999) and strategies that assist a person in achieving a desirable outcome (Halpern, 1997). Paul and Elder (2000) expand this definition by highlighting the autonomy of individuals who display critical thinking skills. They define critical thinking as "self-directed, self-disciplined, self-monitored and self-corrective thinking" (Paul & Elder, 2000, p. 15). Constructivist theories of education (see, for example, Fosnot, 1989) advocate the importance of fostering critical thinking through curricula to equip students with reasoning and analytical skills. Richards (2001) suggests that the responsibility for fostering and nurturing development of critical thinking lies with formal education systems, particularly higher education. Western tertiary education has recognized a need for cultivation of critical thinking in all disciplines; hence, it is a key area in universities' graduate attributes which needs to be embedded in the outcomes and assessment of university courses (Behar-Horenstein & Niu, 2011). Indeed, many higher education programs throughout the world embed opportunities to develop critical thinking skills in discipline-specific teaching, for example, engineering (Niewoehner, 2006) and English-language courses (Thompson, 1999). Recent EAP research and practices have recognized EAP as an appropriate place for the

I. Liyanage & T. Walker (eds.), English for Academic Purposes (EAP) in Asia, 65–77.

development of critical thinking skills while enhancing language learning (Paton, 2011; Thompson, 1999).

Many studies of the acculturation process of Asian students into Western academic culture have revealed that these students encounter various problems in adopting a critical stance in their writing (Durkin, 2008, 2010). Ballard and Clanchy's (1997) deconstruction of pedagogical practices involved in teaching critical thinking skills identifies three main processes: 1) analysis of "complex matter to its simple elements" (Ballard & Clanchy, 1997, p. 32), 2) adoption of a critical attitude by questioning and evaluating, and 3) presentation of a persuasive and reasoned argument. These processes, however, can be difficult in practice due to students' varied intellectual capacities, individual characteristics, and cultural variables. Notwithstanding the limitations of definition, it is argued that critical thinking skills are an essential component in the EAP classroom in an era where learner-centredness and the development of critical pedagogy is at the heart of language education (Jordan, Carlile, & Stack, 2008). As such, many EAP programs around the world see the relevance of embedding critical thinking skills into their curricula and teaching. However, countries with limited resources, such as Sri Lanka, in which English is taught as a second language, face numerous challenges in achieving this. The following is a brief synopsis of the current debates on promoting critical thinking in EAP.

Students in South East Asian countries, such as Sri Lanka, are increasingly required to have cultivated critical thinking skills to meet national and international workforce demands. To align with these needs, EAP teaching has undergone curriculum changes. EAP curricula are typically decided independently by each university and, thus, EAP teachers are entrusted with the responsibility of developing the syllabi and materials for development of language skills and of critical thinking. Secondary and tertiary education institutions use either Sinhala or Tamil as the medium of instruction, with a limited number of universities using English. These differences have an impact on how EAP teachers implement critical thinking practices to meet local needs. The research reported in this chapter investigates teachers' challenges and difficulties in implementing a Western-based critical thinking pedagogy in a Sri Lankan tertiary education setting and examines how EAP practitioners negotiate such challenges in their teaching contexts. The ensuing sections of this chapter provide a review of the literature based on the debates and research on the use of critical thinking in the language classroom and its practice.

LITERATURE REVIEW

EAP has been identified as an appropriate field for teaching critical thinking skills, due to the students' intellectual maturity and their involvement in problem-solving activities that prepare them to enter the job market. There is considerable research that suggests embedding critical thinking skills and activities in EAP facilitates the learning of the four macro-skills (Kamali & Fahim, 2011; Shirkhani & Fahim, 2011; Tama, 1989; Thompson, 1999; Wilson, 2009). Studies by Wilson (2009) and

Kamali and Fahim (2011) show that there is a significant correlation between language learning and critical reading, even if students' language competencies vary significantly. Gaskaree, Mashhady, and Dousti (2010) examined the possibilities of integrating critical thinking activities such as reading journals, reading logs, and literacy portfolios with language-teaching activities. They argued that teaching language items exclusively has limited value in language learning and proposed the integration of critical thinking skills to advance opportunities for language learning. These views are shared by Kabilan (2000, p. 1092) who argued that "learners can only become proficient language users if they, besides using the language and knowing the meaning, could display creative and critical thinking through the language." Kabilan (2000) and Masduqi (2011) suggest that this requires a change in teachers' attitudes and a strong motivation to include students in problem-solving activities. Through an ethnographic observation of a classroom task followed by student interviews, Kiely (2004) studied how critical thinking is integrated in a speaking task in which learners analyze their personal language-learning history. He found that this task was infused with opportunities for learner expression and offers a supportive learning environment. This study suggested that "teacher-led innovation and experimentation in the classroom" (Kiely, 2004, p. 226) is required to enhance critical thinking skills in EAP.

In contrast, numerous studies caution against the use of pedagogies that promote critical thinking skills in EAP classrooms (Dwight Atkinson, 1997; Moore, 2011). Researchers (Dwight Atkinson, 1997; Kramsch, 1993; Pennycook, 2001) alert TESOL practitioners to the challenges posed by the culture-dependent nature of critical thinking due to the claim that it is very difficult for Asian students to demonstrate critical thinking skills in the Western sense. Dwight Atkinson (1997) argues that as social values and norms are culture specific, developing critical thinking skills may be confronting and complex in multicultural EAP classrooms as interpretations depend upon religious and cultural values of learners and teachers. Moore (2011) challenges the idea of critical thinking as a single generic skill with a set process and identifies diverse critical thinking skills activated in different disciplines, such as history, geography, and law. Critical thinking is defined and measured differently in academic disciplines (Moore, 2011), and thus disciplines, and even particular courses, may require a range of tasks and abilities that are dissimilar, so students need to understand these differences to score well in their courses. Moore concludes that core tasks recommended in EAP course-books may be irrelevant for some students.

Dissonance in opinions on the integration of critical thinking skills in the EAP classroom and disparity of opinions about Asian and Western EAP practices stem largely from studies conducted in Western contexts, and involving Asian students studying in Western contexts. EAP education in the Asian context seems to be the target of severe criticisms for a lack of focus on critical thinking, criticisms based on anecdotal evidence and not on empirical evidence or research on Asian practices. There is limited research on critical thinking praxis, and its relevance, in Asian EAP classrooms, and EAP practitioners' perceptions of embedding critical thinking in their teaching, and even less research on EAP practices in the Sri

Lankan context. Given the gap in this research, the purpose of this study was to contribute to the current debate on teaching critical thinking by investigating the perspectives of Sri Lankan EAP practitioners on the challenges and difficulties they face in embedding critical thinking in EAP instruction and the strategies they adopt in negotiating such challenges in their classrooms.

Currently in Sri Lanka, although English language education is deemed integral in meeting local and international demands, many local students encounter difficulties learning English language with limited language resources, as well as limited language exposure (Liyanage, 2012). The majority of university programmes are conducted in Sinhala or Tamil medium, although some faculties in Sri Lankan universities conduct courses in English medium. Despite a common secondary school education, English-language proficiency levels of students vary at entry to university (Liyanage, 2010), and their English language needs at university depend on the university they attend and the courses and programs they choose. For example, to complete programs in medicine and engineering, students require advanced levels of English-language proficiency, especially in reading and writing. Most university English courses are conducted by English Language Teaching Units (ELTUs) in respective faculties that manage and deliver multi-level English-language courses that are either compulsory or optional, depending on the specific courses and programs.

Recently, Sri Lankan universities worked collaboratively towards developing benchmarks, now in place, that align assessments of English-language competency with the Common European Framework Reference (CEFR) (Raheem, 2009). By adapting descriptors from the CEFR, the Sri Lankan EAP benchmarks integrate critical thinking skills in the four macro-skills which include understanding opinions from facts, drawing inferences from academic texts, and distinguishing between formal and informal styles of discourse (Raheem, 2009). Moreover, a careful observation of the Sri Lanka Qualification Framework (SLQF) (Ministry of Higher Education, 2012) adopted in higher education indicates that levels 1 to 10 in tertiary education should aim at developing students' problem-solving and inquiry skills. However, Raheem (2009) identified a number of challenges in the implementation of the Sri Lankan English benchmarks, including the diversity of EAP practices across universities, diversity in class sizes and facilities, and Sri Lankan students' varied entry-level English-language skills and their poor motivation to learn English. More specifically, these circumstances represent obstacles to achievement of benchmarks related to critical thinking. The lack of English-language skills in Sri Lankan students whose linguistic repertoires are dominated by the vernacular languages Tamil and Singhalese (Liyanage, 2010) constrains development of communicative skills and adoption of critical stances in speaking and writing. As noted earlier, the influence on thinking of religions, such as Buddhism and Hinduism, can pose cultural barriers to adoption of Western critical thinking styles (Dwight Atkinson, 1997; Kramsch, 1993; Pennycook, 2001). Empirical studies, such as reported in this chapter, of the responses of local EAP and ELT teachers who face these obstacles and challenges are essential if Sri Lankan EAP teachers are to be equipped with skills and strategies to negotiate teaching of critical thinking and to continue improving the standards of English education. Insights gained from this study can be applied to other EFL contexts with similar constraints and circumstances.

RESEARCH DESIGN

The authors used semi-structured interviews with 10 EAP practitioners to examine their views about the challenges and tensions encountered in negotiating critical thinking practices in EAP classrooms in Sri Lanka. These were organized into three main sections: English-language learner needs, teachers' beliefs about critical thinking, and teachers' difficulties in teaching critical thinking sensitive to local needs.

Invitation letters requesting participation in the study were sent to ELTU units in various Sri Lankan universities. The 10 participants (T1-T10) who volunteered were local teachers with TESOL qualifications obtained mostly from Sri Lankan universities and with experience teaching EAP at postgraduate and undergraduate levels. The interviews were conducted by the researchers via Skype. Technological improvements, such as Skype and emailing, have made such studies possible despite the distance and the lack of opportunity for travel to meet the participants in person (Gaiser & Schreiner, 2009). Interviews were between 30 minutes and 1 hour in duration, were audio-recorded, and were conducted in English and/or Sinhalese, depending on the individual teacher's preference, although most teachers chose English. The recorded interviews were transcribed and subjected to content analysis using deductive and inductive categories to identify common and recurrent themes (see, for example, Mayring, 2000).

RESULTS AND DISCUSSION

A comprehensive examination of the themes emerging from the interviews demonstrated that integrating critical thinking pedagogy in EAP presents several challenges for Sri Lankan teachers. The following discussion focusses on the salient themes emerging from the interview responses: teachers' understanding of and views about the importance of critical thinking and challenges in the application of critical thinking pedagogies.

Teachers' Understanding of Critical Thinking

Due to the complex nature of critical thinking, teachers were asked to provide their own definition and understanding of this concept. The responses demonstrated that all teachers had more or less similar ideas and a solid understanding of critical thinking. The most typical features found in teachers' responses reflected a sequence of steps which comprise the comprehension and analysis of input, reflective thinking by identifying arguments, and reaching logical conclusions or forming opinions based on arguments. Teachers considered the comprehension of the given message as an essential element of critical thinking; this is a major

69

challenge that students encounter in demonstrating critical thinking in the EAP classroom, and central to the ability to analyse and reflect upon given input.

The teachers' perspectives on critical thinking in EAP are consistent with the existing definitions of critical thinking offered by Ballard and Clanchy (1997) and align with Moore's (2011) explanation that critical thinking is not a single generic skill that can be taught prescriptively but comprises multiple abilities activated in different disciplines such as Philosophy, History, and Literary Studies. Moore's (2011) argument that these processes vary is based on careful analysis of assignment tasks given in each discipline, and leads him to the conclusion of the inappropriateness of unifying and teaching critical skills in EAP. However, it is the contention of the researchers that critical thinking tasks in the EAP classroom encourage similar cognitive processes that assist in students' language development and that students could then transfer to other disciplines (Celce-Murcia & Olshtain, 2000).

Teachers who incorporated critical thinking in their EAP teaching were asked to provide examples of tasks to illustrate how they employed it in their practice. Half the teachers who were interviewed provided examples that included writing and reading tasks that involved topics which required the students to identify advantages or disadvantages of important issues, presentation of opinions, and the logical sequence of ideas in an argument, for example, global warming and climate change, freedom of speech, television's influence on family life, and perspectives of Kandy Perahera (a traditional procession in Sri Lanka). These responses suggest that Sri Lankan university teachers have some understanding of how critical thinking can be applied in EAP teaching, but their practice is limited to specific task types. It is possible that teachers may be providing opportunities for development of some skills in students but do not recognize them as promoting critical thinking in activities they use. This is exemplified in one of the teachers' responses:

> We can do it (teach critical thinking) in speaking, no? I do not really know, but when teaching poetry we ask them to think beyond the poem to understand what the poet meant and so on, is this enough? Not sure how you do it. (T6: lines 15-16)

This points to limitations in teachers' capacities for development of appropriate critical thinking pedagogy in their context. We suggest that teachers would benefit from organized training and consultation, not only to develop their understanding of critical thinking skills (for comprehensive lists of these skills, see Celce-Murcia & Olshtain, 2000; Kabilan, 2000; Shirkhani & Fahim, 2011) but also to facilitate reflection on design of practical activities and assessment tasks for integrating critical thinking skills in their language teaching.

Teachers' views about the role of critical thinking in the EAP classroom are complicated. The majority of teachers supported the idea that critical thinking is an essential skill that should be incorporated in EAP teaching and argued that it should be promoted in EAP instruction as it allows students to be active thinkers and autonomous learners:

University education is tertiary education. When a person comes to that level, we need to cultivate their higher order thinking. In the long run, it is an investment to the country. We should help students to think critically not only at university but also from day one. That is how we can progress as a country. (T7: lines 5-7)

However, despite their agreement about the important role of critical thinking, teachers also expressed reservations with regards to the place of critical thinking in the EAP classroom in Sri Lankan universities. Teachers suggested that students' limited English-language skills hinder their understanding or application of critical thinking. Other teachers claimed that critical thinking pedagogy confronts difficulties related to the traditional learning culture of Sri Lankan education. They believed that students' critical thinking abilities are constrained by the fact that they are accustomed to a culture of rote learning and memory-based, product-oriented assessment tasks, and thus students have not experienced questioning, critiquing, or inferencing in the language classroom.

Interestingly, the majority oppose the view that critical thinking is a new concept in the Sri Lankan context, suggesting that they are familiar with the concept and its meaning. In fact, many reportedly include it in their own teaching, although other teachers reported that they have to prioritise the central goal of students' development of the macro-skills. It is clear that teachers welcome the inclusion of critical thinking in the EAP classroom but are confronted with certain challenges that constrain their embrace of what they believe to be appropriate and productive pedagogy. Negotiation of EAP practice that embeds critical thinking skills requires careful navigation of tensions arising from the intersection of institutional demands and learner needs and capacities in the local sociocultural context. Restrictions imposed by the respective faculties on the teaching of macro-skills and lack of university policy are some of the many challenges that teachers confront and are discussed in more detail in the next section.

Integrating Critical Thinking Practices in the Sri Lankan EAP Classroom

The current study explored teachers' perceptions of practices, and possible challenges, in their integration of critical thinking practices in EAP classrooms. The majority of teachers rejected the idea that Sri Lankan university students are not good at critical thinking, thus disconfirming suggestions in other research (Egege & Kutieleh, 2004). However, teachers identified a number of challenges in their efforts to incorporate critical thinking tasks in their EAP classrooms.

The most critical problem thought to influence students' understanding and development of critical thinking was English-language proficiency. EAP classes in Sri Lankan universities usually consist of students of varied levels of proficiency and, in these multilevel classes, addressing students' language difficulties and needs dominates teaching time. While some advanced-level students can manage set tasks reasonably well, others confront various problems due to limited vocabulary and grammar competence. It was noted that limited vocabulary knowledge and partial understanding of the meaning of complex grammatical structures interfere with students' achievement of certain tasks and their self-expression. Lack of understanding of input may lead to students' inability to understand the coherence of texts in reading tasks and to develop arguments in response, thus impeding development of critical thinking skills. Teacher 5 cited an example of an essay topic, "Does television deprive children's family time?," that students had to discuss in class, arguing that students found it difficult, as it required good command of language for students to make an argument. These findings are consistent with Kumaravadivelu's (2003) argument which suggests that limited language skills can disable students' abilities in critical thinking. While some teachers in the study struggled to respond to this fundamental problem of students' proficiency, others thrived on the challenge, adopting various strategies, for example, modifying and simplifying language in textbook activities to accommodate students' language levels. Some participants adopted a bilingual approach in which teachers encourage students to use their mother tongue, Sinhalese or Tamil, in addition to English when they have issues in relation to vocabulary. This method is consistent with Canagarajah's (2006) suggestion that bilingual writing is a pedagogical and strategic tool to assist language improvement and self-expression. Bilingual language models have been shown to maximize language learning when students are allowed to employ skills from both languages (Creese & Blackledge, 2010; Hornberger, 2002) and could be seen as a scaffolding tool in the students' development of critical thinking skills (David Atkinson, 1987).

Given their acknowledgement of the centrality of critical thinking in language teaching and learning, teachers need to not only increase the range of activities used to teach critical thinking, but also embed these in language learning tasks. We argue that critical thinking-focussed tasks involving knowledge and/or skills such as genre, generalizing, summarizing, coherence, and cohesion, and in which students engage in thinking beyond language learning, are good platforms to promote, motivate, and stimulate language acquisition and increase students' language competence (Daud & Husin, 2004).

Teachers identified lack of consistent attention to critical thinking in EAP syllabi/curricula as another significant obstacle to integration of critical thinking:

> We have a syllabus we also have the flexibility to use our resources from internet. I create my own tasks for them to do. We haven't got much information about critical thinking not many teachers are aware of the need. (T2: lines 40-43)

As well as improving English-language skills, EAP programs are required to support major disciplines and faculties. Demands to assist students in meeting disciplinary language needs constrain teacher practices and minimize freedom to choose materials. Teachers are often asked to focus on development of macro-skills, which creates tensions between their beliefs, and the needs and expectations of students. The inconsistency in EAP curricula in Sri Lankan education has generated confusion and insecurity among teachers about their roles as English-language teachers and uncertainty about the role of critical thinking in the development of language skills. Teachers' assertions that "we are language teachers" (T1: line 15), "our focus is on teaching the language" (T6, line 2), "our role is to improve their English" (T9: line 16) and "we are not asked to do it?" (T8: line 15) reflect the dilemma they experience over the question of whether critical thinking skills are one of their teaching objectives. As further evidence of this confusion and uncertainty at the time of the interviews, only one participant was aware of the CEFR-aligned benchmarks for assessment in EAP which are now in place. This could be attributed to lack of effective communication between curriculum developers, managers, and EAP teachers in hierarchical education systems. Miscommunications, such as these, need to be addressed in order to support teachers to practice confidently with a clear understanding of the aims and objectives of EAP programs. There should be systematic methods to disseminate materials and policy documents between teachers and managers. In addition, as Liyanage (2012) explains, hierarchical systems need reforms to allow flexibility to foster shared decision making by students and teachers.

Despite the confusion around inclusion of critical thinking skills in EAP curricula, most interviewees agreed on the necessity to enhance students' critical thinking skills to meet professional expectations and global needs. For this reason, it may be necessary that policies and curricula are developed at a national level to incorporate critical thinking as a main goal. This needs to be accompanied by systematic and appropriate teacher training to equip teachers to teach critical thinking skills. Thompson (1999) and Masduqi (2011) have offered useful recommendations for integrating critical thinking skills in language classrooms that can benefit teachers. It is important to acknowledge that teacher training should be relevant and sensitive to local Sri Lankan practices. Teaching materials should embed cultural values to assist teachers in developing their critical pedagogy: "effective pedagogies are best home grown" (Liyanage, 2012, p. 147), otherwise they can lead to teacher and learner alienation and decrease student motivation.

Additional challenges facing teachers in implementing pedagogies that promote critical thinking skills are students' lack of motivation and poor attendance in EAP classes. Most teachers thought the time allocated for EAP in some universities was inadequate because students needed more classroom time. More than that, English classes offered at the university level are not compulsory for all students, and it was noted that students tend to channel their energy to their content courses, allocating little time to English-language classes. Hence, EAP classes are poorly attended. Limited classroom time and low or infrequent attendance make teachers attend to students' basic language needs such as reading comprehension and vocabulary development.

Efforts to integrate critical thinking practices in EAP pedagogy are also complicated by students' educational experiences in primary and secondary schooling, which are characterized by rote learning, focus on memorization, and exam-oriented assessment. Participants attributed students' continued dependence on teacher instruction and direction, and reluctance to engage in problem-solving activities, to this traditional learning culture. Teachers complained that they encounter resistance in students' attitudes and find it difficult to stimulate and motivate them: "Mostly they are taught to memorize and produce knowledge in exams" (T1, line 8). This suggests that teachers may need to develop techniques for accommodating students' culture in learning activities that promote critical thinking. Participants discussed employment of various activities, such as brainstorming, to stimulate students' critical thinking. Teacher 7 (lines 18-21), for example, described a brainstorming task based on the traditional Kandy Perahera, a festival which includes a procession of people with elegant costumes and adorned elephants, an ancient custom established to worship Gods and kings. Many students would think only about a description of the festival, but they were encouraged to criticize its importance and develop their own reactions to this historical event, focussing on different perspectives such as history and feudalism, caste and class system, and social changes from past to present.

Significantly, Teacher 7 allows students to use their first language and code-switch when they encounter expression difficulties. Such resourceful and knowledgeable teachers can negotiate and minimize problems surrounding integration of critical thinking activities in the classroom, but although many teachers accept the challenge on a personal level, and have the confidence and the creativity to resolve such difficulties, there are political, institutional, and administrative challenges, such as lack of time, incomplete policy, and discipline-specific needs, which reduce their freedom and constrain the effectiveness of responses. Within the context of globalization and shift in educational practices, these issues need to be taken seriously in the Sri Lankan university system. Appropriate teacher development and provision of culturally relevant materials can assist teachers in understanding and executing their teaching roles.

Participants perceived students to have passive and respectful attitudes in the classroom and to experience feelings of embarrassment in presenting their opinion and negotiating solutions. This, the teachers explained, is not indicative of students' lack of ability to critique, but a result of Buddhist practices and cultural beliefs of showing respect and politeness to teachers. Two teachers (T1 & T2) mentioned that they strive to develop democratic classroom environments, nurturing friendly relationships between teachers and students so that students can overcome such anxieties and feel supported to critique and express opinions, while respecting the views of others. Another sociocultural issue was the lack of culturally relevant material to teach critical thinking. For examples, topics such as same-sex marriage or living together can be inappropriate and sensitive in the Sri Lankan context. Some teachers, particularly Teachers 7 and 10, said that they modify some activities found in Western textbooks to provide culturally appropriate discussion topics and to negate student inhibition.

CONCLUSION

This chapter focussed on a small number of EAP teachers who volunteered to participate in this project. In order to provide in-depth insight into teachers' perceptions, and for generalization purposes, further studies need to be conducted with larger samples. Nevertheless, it contributes to our understanding of tensions in

EAP instruction, calling for practices that address the multilingual realities of Sri Lanka and other Asian contexts, as well as their diverse academic language needs. It explored also the challenges Sri Lankan teachers experience in integrating critical thinking skills in their programs and how they address these challenges while identifying tensions and challenges that need to be addressed. Future research could examine students' and teachers' perceptions of their understanding of critical thinking and EAP in diverse Asian cultural contexts.

In the age of globalization, English language education plays a significant role in developing students' intercultural skills to function as global citizens. Critical thinking is a central component of these skills and thus an important goal of EAP. It is important therefore that the use of culturally appropriate resources and teacher training be facilitated within relevant educational policy directives. This will strengthen and enhance practitioners' ability to better negotiate critical thinking activities appropriate for their context.

ACKNOWLEDGEMENTS

We would like to thank the participants who volunteered to be interviewed and made this study possible. Our gratitude also goes to the two anonymous reviewers and the editors of this volume for their useful comments which helped in revising this chapter.

REFERENCES

Atkinson, David. (1987). The mother tongue in the classroom: A neglected resource? *ELT Journal, 41*(4), 241-247.

Atkinson, Dwight. (1997). A critical approach to critical thinking in TESOL. *TESOL Quarterly, 31*(1), 71-94.

Ballard, B., & Clanchy, J. (1997). *Study abroad: A manual for Asian students* (Revised ed.). Kuala Lumpur, Malaysia: Longman.

Behar-Horenstein, L. S., & Niu, L. (2011). Teaching critical thinking skills in higher education: A review of the literature. *Journal of College Teaching and Learning, 8*(2), 25-42.

Canagarajah, A. S. (2006). Toward a writing pedagogy of shuttling between languages: Learning from multilingual writers. *College English, 68*(6), 589-604.

Celce-Murcia, M., & Olshtain, E. (2000). *Discourse and context in language teaching.* Oxford, UK: Oxford University Press.

Creese, A., & Blackledge, A. (2010). Translanguaging in the bilingual classroom: A pedagogy for learning and teaching? *The Modern Language Journal, 94*(1), 103-115.

Daud, N. M., & Husin, Z. (2004). Developing critical thinking skills in computer-aided extended reading classes. *British Journal of Educational Technology, 35*(4), 477-487.

Durkin, K. (2008). The middle way: East Asian master's students' perceptions of critical argumentation in UK universities. *Journal of Studies in International Education, 12*(1), 38-55.

Durkin, K. (2010). The adaptation of East Asian master's students to western norms of critical thinking and argumentation in the UK. *Intercultural Education, 19*(1), 15-27.

Egege, S., & Kutieleh, S. (2004). Critical thinking: Teaching foreign notions to foreign students. *International Education Journal, 4*(4), 75-85.

Ennis, R. H. (1989). Critical thinking and subject specificity: Clarification and needed research. *Educational Researcher, 18*(3), 4-10.

Fosnot, C. T. (1989). *Enquiring teachers, enquiring learners: A constructivist approach for teaching.* New York: Teachers College Press.

Gaiser, T. J., & Schreiner, A. E. (2009). *A guide to conducting online research.* London: Sage Publications.

Gaskaree, B. L., Mashhady, H., & Dousti, M. (2010). Using critical thinking activities as tools to integrate language skills. *Sino-US English Teaching, 7*(4), 33-45.

Halpern, D. J. (1997). *Critical thinking across the curriculum.* Mahwah, NJ: Lawrence Erlbaum Associates.

Hornberger, N. H. (2002). Multilingual language policies and the continua of biliteracy: An ecological approach. *Language Policy, 1*(1), 27-51.

Jordan, A., Carlile, O., & Stack, A. (2008). *Approaches to learning: A guide for educators.* Glasgow, UK: Bell and Bain.

Kabilan, M. K. (2000). Creative and critical thinking in language classrooms. *The Internet TESL Journal, VI*(6). http://iteslj.org/Techniques/Kabilan-CriticalThinking.html

Kamali, Z., & Fahim, M. (2011). The relationship between critical thinking ability of Iranian EFL learners and their resilience level facing unfamiliar vocabulary items in reading. *Journal of Language Teaching and Research, 2*(1), 104-111.

Kiely, R. (2004). Learning to critique in EAP. *Journal of English for Academic Purposes, 3*(3), 211-227.

Kramsch, C. (1993). *Context and culture.* Oxford: Oxford University Press.

Kumaravadivelu, B. (2003). Problematizing cultural stereotypes in TESOL. *TESOL Quarterly, 37*(4), 709-719.

Liyanage, I. (2010). Globalisation: Medium-of-instruction policy, indigenous educational systems and ELT in Sri Lanka. In V. Vaish (Ed.), *Globalization of language and culture in Asia* (pp. 209-232). London: Continuum.

Liyanage, I. (2012). Critical pedagogy in ESL/EFL teaching in South-east Asia: Practices and challenges with examples from Sri Lanka. In K. Sung & R. Pederson (Eds.), *Critical ELT practices in Asia: Key issues, practices, and possibilities* (pp. 137-152). Rotterdam, the Netherlands: Sense Publishers.

Masduqi, H. (2011). Critical thinking skills and meaning in English language teaching. *TEFLIN Journal, 22*(2), 185-200.

Mayring, P. (2000). Qualitative content analysis. *Forum: Qualitative Social Research, 1*(2). http://nbn-resolving.de/urn:nbn:de:0114-fqs0002204

Ministry of Higher Education. (2012). *Sri Lanka qualifications framework.* Colombo, Sri Lanka: Retrieved from http://www.ugc.ac.lk/en/all-notices/1156-sri-lanka-qualifications-framework.html.

Moore, T. J. (2011). Critical thinking and disciplinary thinking: A continuing debate. *Higher Education Research & Development, 30*(3), 261-274.

Niewoehner, R. J. (2006). Applying a critical thinking model for engineering education. *World Transactions on Engineering and Technology Education, 5*(2), 341-344.

Paton, M. (2011). Asian students, critical thinking and English as an academic lingua franca. *Analytic Teaching and Philosophical Praxis, 32*(1), 27-39.

Paul, R., & Elder, L. (2000). Critical thinking: Nine strategies for everyday life, Part I. *Journal of Developmental Education, 24*(1), 40-41.

Pennycook, A. (2001). *Critical applied linguistics: A critical introduction.* Mahwah, NJ: Lawrence Erlbaum.

Raheem, R. (2009). *Establishing benchmarks in academic English: The Sri Lankan experience.* Paper presented at the 7th Asia TEFL Conference, Bangkok, Thailand.

Richards, J. C. (2001). *Curriculum development in language teaching.* Cambridge, UK: Cambridge University Press.

Shirkhani, S., & Fahim, M. (2011). *Enhancing critical thinking in foreign language learners.* Paper presented at the 1st International Conference on Foreign Language Teaching and Applied Linguistics, Sarajevo, Bosnia and Herzegovina, 5-7 May.

Tama, M. C. (1989). Critical thinking has a place in every classroom. *Journal of Reading, 33*(1), 64-65.

Thompson, C. (1999). *Critical thinking: What is it and how do we teach it in English for Academic Purposes (EAP) programs?* Paper presented at the HERDSA Annual International Conference, Melbourne, Australia, 12-15 July.

Walker, P., & Finney, N. (1999). Skill development and critical thinking in higher education. *Teaching in Higher Education, 4*(4), 531-547.

Wilson, K. (2009). *Reading in the margins: EAP reading pedagogies and their critical, postcritical potential.* Unpublished doctoral dissertation, University of Sydney.

Maya Gunawardena
Learning and Teaching Group
University of New South Wales, Canberra
Australia

Eleni Petraki
Discipline of Humanities
Faculty of Arts and Design
University of Canberra
Australia

RAQIB CHOWDHURY & MUNASIR KAMAL

6. BALANCING CONFORMITY AND EMPOWERMENT

Critical Needs Analysis in an EAP course at Dhaka University

INTRODUCTION

Pragmatism, as understood in the context of English for Academic Purposes (EAP), refers to teacher and learner subjectivities in a context-sensitive approach to EAP curriculum (Allison, 1996). Such context-sensitive pragmatic approaches consider day-to-day practicalities and constraints with regard to the challenges of, and what is truly achievable within, any given EAP program. From a critical needs analysis perspective, EAP practice is an essentially pragmatic undertaking which requires an optimized understanding of local contexts and the needs of particular cohorts of students. However, studies of EAP, which are predominantly local and regional even when it comes to international contributions, often narrowly align with a handful of accepted EAP research and discourse traditions originating from Britain and North America as accepted centres of influence (Flowerdew & Peacock, 2001). Such reductionist perspectives necessitate greater diversity in research approaches and scopes, as well as international dialogues looking into disparate research traditions and curricular concerns in EAP across cultures and regions.

Bangladesh is ethnolinguistically homogeneous with 98.8% of its population speaking Bangla or Bengali (Bangladesh Bureau of Statistics, 2012). From the "despised instrument of the colonizers" (Chowdhury & Farooqui, 2011, p. 148) reminiscent of a long colonial history, English has now become an indispensable instrument readily associated with material and social success for Bangladeshi people. This is significant for EAP learners and practitioners as proficiency in English is a factor in increasing the likelihood of pursing higher education and, by extension, lucrative employment, professional advancement, and social prestige, all widely seen as inevitable and desirable results of being proficient in English (Hu, 2005). Such extrinsic motivation has led a substantial number of Bangladeshis to master a form of correct English, especially given that studying through the medium of English is a matter of great importance. In order to meet this demand, there has been an increase in investments in English literacies by successive governments across all levels of education in Bangladesh (Chowdhury & Kabir, forthcoming). The offering of EAP courses for undergraduate students by many public universities is one such initiative, and the Foundation Course in English (FC), a first-year compulsory EAP course for English undergraduate students in the Department of English at the Dhaka University, is a specific example of this.

I. Liyanage & T. Walker (eds.), English for Academic Purposes (EAP) in Asia, 79–92.

Over the past 15 years, the FC at Dhaka University has undergone major changes from a generic EAP course to a deregulated, decentralized, and more discipline-specific offering to suit the needs of the English Department. However, it has also been criticized as what Benesch (2001) calls accommodationist, in its attempt to fit students within the Department's perceived objectives of manufacturing a premeditated product, rather than fostering students' literacy in the conventions of English-language academic discourses necessary to understand their disciplines and successfully navigate their learning, and, most importantly, empowering them through the appropriation of a diversity of academic literacies. Despite a handful of studies conducted on the FC to date (see Chaudhury, 2011; Chowdhury, 2003; Chowdhury & Le Ha, 2008; Khan, 2000), questions about certain aspects of the EAP curriculum, including the need for needs analysis, learner autonomy, student empowerment, and teacher enfranchisement, have remained unanswered. More specifically, whether and how the notion of critical pedagogy has been operationalized in FC to fulfil the stated objectives of the course in a locally sensitive manner is a matter that has not been researched empirically.

The pedagogy of English teaching in Bangladesh has long been characterised by grammar-translation, aligning comfortably with, and fuelled by, a strong reliance on the security of rote learning of grammatical rules and memorisation of vocabulary, translation of (mostly decontextualized) text, and written exercises at all levels. Chowdhury and Farooqui (2011) report how, throughout school education to the higher secondary level, students in Bangladesh are brought up on a heavy diet of grammatical rules and student activities involving mostly mechanical drills. The main problem with such pedagogy has been that students are encouraged to learn the language but not how to use it (Hasan, 2004). With memorisation widely accepted and acknowledged, speaking and listening skills are avoided and never assessed. The resultant effect implicates not only student competence at the tertiary level, but also students' expectations of a course such as the FC. Due to teaching and learning experienced at the higher secondary level, students are not quite prepared for the more complex demands of teaching and learning in English at the tertiary level, a situation further exacerbated at Dhaka University due to lack of any needs analysis mechanism in place. Such a scenario is an opportunity for curriculum makers and practitioners to consider what a critical-pragmatic approach can offer.

This chapter uses ideas expressed collectively by the teaching staff of Department of English at Dhaka University, as well as curriculum artefacts, to describe the Foundation Course in English (FC) in order to problematize the usefulness of the essentially Western notion of critical needs analysis in the Bangladeshi educational setting. It looks at how, in calibrating the course, a new generation of Western-trained teachers have been challenged in their attempts to emphasize the process-oriented teaching and learning approaches over product-oriented practices. In doing so, this chapter does not deal with the politics of English in general, or the nature of EAP content development in the FC; rather, it looks at how, through the interface of FC teachers' and students' teaching and learning, needs analysis is understood and how FC pedagogy aligns with the notion of critical pragmatism within a tertiary education context in Bangladesh.

Pragmatism in EAP

The notion of pragmatism, when associated with EAP, has been understood as an instrument that facilitates conformity by fitting students into mostly unquestioned acceptance of subordinate roles that sustain an "educational status quo" (Allison, 1996, p. 85). In the 1990s, researchers in EAP such as Benesch (1996) and Pennycook (1990, 1994a, 1994b) singled out the ideological implications of pragmatic views of English language teaching as problematic. What was widely accepted as the primary motivation behind EAP – the aim of development of academic communicative competence (Swales, 1990) – was criticized as forcing ideological conformity in the name of pragmatism. EAP pragmatism paradoxically denies both learners and teachers their own voices within a dominant culture. Benesch (1993, p. 711) argues that

> ... the self-professed pragmatism of many EAP advocates ... actually indicates an accommodationist ideology, an endorsement of traditional academic teaching and of current power relations in academia and in society ... (that) ... aims to assimilate ESL students uncritically into academic life ...

Similarly, Pennycook (1994a, pp. 120-121) accuses the pragmatic approach of being reductionist, arguing that "the possibilities of dealing with broader social, cultural or political contexts of discourse are denied by appeal to an ideology of pragmatism" (p. 89). Allison (1996, p. 92) explains that the "inherently conformist" philosophy of EAP pragmatism stems from its failure to see students as individuals with idiosyncratic learning needs, and that such an approach "conspicuously fail(s) to do justice to what prominent (pragmatic) EAP writers have been saying and doing for more than two decades." He argues that a pragmatic willingness to recognize and investigate the diversity of goals, strategies and contexts attendant with EAP experience will be unproductive without the prerequisite categorisation of EAP pragmatism and practice into either conformist or reformist forms.

Allison (1996), however, challenges the notion of EAP pragmatism as a unified, unproblematic, and monolithic ideology that offers support to the status quo of existing power relations in education and society. He proposes as an alternative that "pragmatically inclined EAP practitioners and scholars seek to contextualize their understanding and action... in order to pursue educational goals that they value within possibilities and constraints that they identify" (p. 99). Of these, some could facilitate major curricular changes while others could seek to elevate educational opportunities through "subtle adjustments to practice" (p. 99). Although it is common in academic literature to explore whether, and how, specific EAP initiatives are serving powerful interests which conveniently favoured certain changes against others which are obstructed (Allison, 1996; Ivanič, 1998; Pennycook, 1994a), such approach is not helpful in presupposing that EAP teachers are not aware of such possibilities. Rather than a pragmatic approach, which sees learners as homogenous, passive, and accommodating recipients of learning, it is more useful to adopt a critical approach.

Critical Pedagogy to Critical EAP

Across a range of EAP settings, literature (see Crosling & Ward, 2002; Evans, 2010; Hua & Beverton, 2013; Kassim & Ali, 2010; Lobo & Gurney, 2013) has identified widespread mismatch between short-term needs of undergraduate students, both from English and non-English majors, and expectations of what they have learnt when subsequently seeking employment. In addition, as Allison (1996) argues, most EAP initiatives operate within and presuppose a context, rather than holistically reviewing an entire system and the interests it serves. Often, by ignoring wider factors of socio-political importance, they ignore the learners' most important needs. For example, at Dhaka University the concern for helping students through the FC course to successfully navigate their way through five years of education and beyond is an important educational commitment. Rather than conveniently presupposing the status quo of a "fixed" course of study, it is important too to ascertain students' needs and challenges, as well as learning opportunities, through sustained and systematic needs analysis and critical pedagogy.

Along with Pennycook (1990), Benesch (2001) is one of the best-known exponents of critical pedagogy. In juxtaposing EAP and critical pedagogy, her starting point is that EAP has predominantly defined itself as a pedagogic service where teaching programs reflect the features of the disciplines for which L2 students are headed. She calls this stance accommodationist, that is, obsessively sensitive in aligning itself to institutional policies, explaining that EAP should go beyond its preoccupation "to prepare students unquestioningly for institutional expectations" (Benesch, 2001, p. 23). Benesch encourages EAP practitioners, in delivering academic courses, to see their primary role as turning their learners into agents of change through an ethos that emphasizes collectivism rather than individualism as a response to social issues. She argues:

> ... without an analysis of the underlying motivation and goals, it is impossible for ESP teachers to come to terms with the ethics of their practice, to ask who they are working for, and to examine possible consequences of their teaching. (Benesch, 2001, p. 27)

Benesch (2001) further explains that, through its sensitivity to context, EAP is now expected to include, rather than mere linguistic analysis, the view of texts and of knowledge as socially constructed. A critical pedagogy perspective problematizes such a stance and addresses "the politics of teaching, including funding, curricular choices, roles ascribed to teachers and students, and the goals of English teaching in institutions and societies" (Benesch, 2001, p. 41). Indeed, her emphasis on context originates from the recognition of two subjectivities – of multiple identities and institutional hierarchies. By counter-posing the term "rights analysis" as an agent (and prerequisite) for change and learner empowerment, she critiques the widely accepted canons of needs analysis. Her argument is that, in academic scholarship, EAP has been predominantly accommodationist and to counter this, she proposes a critical stance to problematize the approach. She pushes the need for greater acknowledgement of how EAP practitioners are politically conscious in the ways in which they often fight against institutions for the rights of students from non-native English speaking backgrounds. As an alternative, Benesch (2009) proposes the notion of critical EAP (CEAP) (see also Hall, 2000, as discussed later), which takes a more inclusive view of academic purposes by considering the socio-political context of teaching and learning. This is done by considering the intricacies of EAP teachers' and students' social identities, such as race, age, gender, and ethnicities, alongside the obvious and immediate contexts of academic genres and classroom dynamics.

The Critical and the Pragmatic

At this point, we inevitably ask: What categories of pedagogy are involved in EAP? Harwood and Hadley (2004) identify three distinct approaches – the critical approach, the pragmatic approach, and the critical-pragmatic approach. According to Johns (1993, p. 274), pragmatism entails the goal of "prepar(ing) ESL/EFL and native-speaking students for the literacy demands at the secondary or college/university level." Accordingly, pragmatic EAP is basically an instrumental and skills-based approach that teaches students the principal conventions (mostly Anglo-American) of academic discourse norms rather than obliging schools to adapt to L2 students' rhetorical styles and writing to allow them to be able to appropriate these same conventions. Critical EAP, on the other hand, is concerned with "critiquing existing educational institutions and practices, and subsequently transforming both education and society" (Hall, 2000, p. 3). The popularity of CEAP has traditionally been attributed to its insistent questioning of discourse norms. From this critical perspective, the pragmatic approach to EAP falls short of attempting to question the need for reinforcing these predominant norms. Through its insistence on conformity, academic conventions are viewed as inherently naïve and value-neutral, and therefore worthy of imitation. A critical approach takes the cautiously sceptical stance of viewing existing practices as propagating the status quo against peripheral power groups, such as L2 learners of English. Dominant discursive conventions in writing are not dismissed or ignored as natural, rather as "naturalized … the product of relations of power" (Ivanič, 1998, p. 81). It is in this sense that pragmatic EAP views the learner as passive and accommodating.

Both critical and pragmatic EAP practices have been accused, however differently, of prescriptivism (Harwood & Hadley, 2004) – the doctrinal demand and concern for "good," "proper," or "correct" usage and the emphasis on languages as we would like them to be, rather than as we find them. Many critics view CEAP as overtly reactionary due to its insistent interrogation of accepted discourse conventions forcing learners to reject well-accepted practices. Pragmatic EAP, too, can be seen as equally dogmatic in its expectation that all learners should conform to established practices. A critical-pragmatic approach to EAP, on the other hand, synthesizes these two seemingly irreconcilable approaches by acknowledging the importance and necessity of students' exposure to the norms of dominant discourses/conventions and at the same time, like CEAP, emphasizing the value of students having their own choices and freedom in either adopting or rejecting these dominant forms based on their own independent choices. To this extent, the critical-pragmatic approach inherently carries the dual, somewhat conflicting, mission of helping students do well in their studies, and at the same time also encouraging them to take a sceptical approach to the type of education on offer for them (Benesch, 2001, p. xvii) – an aspect that will be discussed later in this chapter.

Pennycook (1994b) explains that his role as critical educator requires him to go beyond helping students just achieve "success" as defined by the institute, and actively facilitate their very understanding of success and rethink about possibilities within their course of study. Rather than endorsing total freedom for students in decision making, he advocates the need to first of all make language linked to social and economic prestige available to students and then to problematize how different standards can present different statuses and possibilities. By incorporating these two approaches through a deliberate adoption of the critical-pragmatic approach in teaching, the vulnerabilities of pragmatism can be avoided.

The Foundation Course and ENG101

The FC was first introduced in 1998 at the tertiary level to all first-year undergraduate students at Dhaka University. It had the dual objective in its capacity as an EAP offering of providing students with English-language skills optimized to help them adapt to the linguistic demands made by their respective academic disciplines, and to develop competence sufficient to find suitable employment opportunities in the job market, which increasingly required English proficiency. Hence, the FC textbook, *Advancing English Skills*, published by the English Department, Dhaka University, contained practical and job-oriented units such as "Writing Resumes," "The Role of English in the 21st Century," and "Effective Business Letters," as well as units on "Writing Paragraphs," "Writing Essays," "Acknowledging Sources" etcetera to help students develop their academic skills. Initially this course was taught twice a week with 50 minutes per class. At inception about 1300 students were enrolled in this course from all the 14 departments of the Faculty of Arts.

A conspicuous departure from the traditional EAP course in Bangladesh, the FC was primarily skills based and had aimed to develop the four macroskills of listening, speaking, reading, and writing, although due to the lack of technology in the classroom and the Arts Faculty's rigid assessment system, instructors soon found themselves having to prioritize reading and writing over listening and speaking – a classic washback phenomena. The FC syllabus was more or less notional; the fundamental units were based on meanings and concepts expressed through the language and not on grammatical items. At the end of the academic year, students sat for the FC exit examination totalling 100 marks of which 33 marks were required to pass. Marks above 50 were added to the final BA Honours result, providing additional incentives for students.

At the bottom of FC's list of priorities was the need to build knowledge around what was perceived as traditional, course-based academic and study needs. Theoretically, at the initial stages, the implementation of the FC represented an innovation in foreign-language learning as continual attempts were made to modify the syllabus content, textbook design, and classroom teaching approaches according to then-current principles of communicative language teaching (Khan, 2000). Over the last 15 years a number of modifications were made to the FC, largely based on ideas developed during several ELT workshops jointly organized by DU and Warwick University, UK for FC teachers as well as a number of studies and reports conducted exclusively on the FC (see for example Chaudhury, 2011; Chowdhury, 2003; Hamid, 2000; Khan, 2000).

An ENG101 teacher who has been teaching this course since its inception (as FC) in 1998 pointed out that most of the current concerns of teaching staff revolve around one central issue – that no real needs analysis had been carried out prior to designing the FC syllabus and that although it was a "CLT [communicative language teaching] syllabus, there was very little understanding of what that entailed at the policy level." She lamented that despite the textbook having a generous number of listening and speaking exercises, there really was no way of testing these valuable skills in the exams. Such "mismatch," she pointed out, was very demotivating for students.

Another teacher pointed out that the course has traditionally been "too ambitious" in its attempt in successfully bringing together "too many students from too many departments" which presupposed the practicality of delivering one standardised course to a diverse and highly mixed-ability group. Such grouping, she argued, defeated the purpose of the FC to cater to the individual needs of students. According to yet another teacher, the course was trying to "achieve too much at the same time." She was critical of the "too large" gap between the proficiency level of most students at the beginning of the course and their expected target at the end of this one-year course.

In response to such shortcomings, particularly the difficulty in meeting the needs of students of heterogeneous abilities from various departments through a single and unified English unit, the Arts Faculty decided to abandon the centralized offering of FC in 2006. This decision coincided with another major change in the faculty that replaced a single academic year with two semesters. The various departments in the Arts Faculty were now granted the freedom to decide whether or not they would offer FC courses to students in their first semester, as well as the content of the course. The English Department was no longer responsible for staffing all English FC classes throughout the Arts Faculty, but the different departments could now employ an instructor of their preference. In 1998, a Bangla language FC course was introduced along with the English FC course. However, with the decentralization of the FC, almost all departments decided to withdraw the

Bangla FC but retain the English FC, perhaps because of the relative importance of English and its perceived instrumental utility in the job market. Meanwhile, many departments in the Science Faculty had also started offering EAP courses. Many departments in both faculties employed teachers from the English Department as part-time instructors to teach their students, though some departments also chose English teachers from other universities. In an accommodationist move, the English syllabus in these other departments was modified to align with the discipline-specific content taught in those departments and with the perceived needs of the students, although no needs analysis was carried out at this stage to justify or support such an approach, for example an ad hoc inclusion of "lab reports" and "presentation skills" in the syllabus was made by an English instructor teaching in the Science Faculty.

The English FC continued to be taught in the English Department at Dhaka University as "English 101." However, despite the rebranding there were a few differences between the defunct English FC and the new English 101. *Advancing English Skills* continued to be used in English 101, although now teachers supplemented the FC textbook with certain chapters from Murphy's (2007) *Intermediate English Grammar*, Langan's (2012) *English Skills*, as well as self-developed materials. During the FC phase, teachers had no option but to teach according to the common syllabus for all departments in the Arts Faculty, whereas the syllabus for English 101 provided greater flexibility. The English 101 syllabus also allowed incoming students, numbering as many as 180 in recent years, to be allocated into four mixed-ability groups, each assigned to a different instructor. Since the beginning of English 101, the four instructors would meet at the beginning of each semester to decide on the course content and structure for that term. While the FC had not allotted points for class participation, 10% of the total points were reserved for attendance and participation in English 101. The remaining 30% and 60% of marks were allotted for mid- and end-semester examinations, respectively. Instructors now had the freedom to involve students in various activities for participation points. They could ask students to do oral presentations and involve them in games and debates which provided students with opportunities for practising speaking. For example, one of the teachers currently teaching English 101, who insisted on the integration of the four skills in the language learning process, regularly took a CD player to class so that her students could practice listening and speaking using *Headway* (Philpot, Curnick, Pathare, Pathare, & Harrison, 2011) materials.

Nonetheless, 90% of the course was still assessed through the university's written exam system, and English 101 continued to remain essentially accommodationist in its approach. From its inception as English FC, it had accepted the role of English as an instrument in attaining higher education and securing a desirable job, and had adapted itself to the Arts Faculty's resource-constrained classrooms and problematic evaluation system. It did not, and still does not, analyze the connection between itself and broader social, economic, and political issues; rather, it takes its position as provider of EAP as inevitable. Instructors of English 101 have relatively more autonomy now than instructors of

English FC did in the past, and they also have control over participation points and can include and implement changes as they see fit during the meeting at the start of each semester. However, they must still work within the mundane practicalities and constraints, which limit what is really possible within the scope of this EAP programme.

In 2010, the English Department of Dhaka University won an award of Taka 9,384,000 (AU$135,000) under the University Grant Commission's Higher Education Quality Enhancement Project (HEQEP), which, among other reforms, made it possible for the department to revise the contents of English 101. The project spanned two years from February 2011 to February 2013 and, according to the project proposal, funds from this award were used for:
- Capacity building in the leading English department in Bangladesh to improve teaching and learning for enrolled learners
- Imparting ICT skills to students and making optimum use of new technology
- Ensuring student-centred, need-based, and up-to-date pedagogy
- Teacher development for curriculum implementation
- Producing more employable graduates for the global market

This award allowed the department to consider changes that had been impractical and unthinkable for so long. A series of workshops and teacher-training sessions were organized, and the Department decided to revise its published course books, which included modifying *Advancing English Skills* to meet the specific needs of English Department students. Teachers discussed the limitations of the existing textbook and agreed on units that were not working well in class because they were not adequately challenging for students of the English Department. For example, the unit *Advancing English Skills* had been designed initially for the entire Arts Faculty during the FC phase, where, generally speaking, the students of other departments were not as proficient in English as students of the English Department. In implementing the project, the department – for the first time – conducted needs analyses in which approximately 350 participants comprising current and former students of English 101 categorized certain units of the textbook as less or more useful and suggested changes to the syllabus that they thought would help future students. Interestingly, while teachers were more concerned with redesigning *Advancing English Skills*, students expressed less concern with the book, and more concern with the scope of teaching, such as incorporating speaking practice in English 101, mainly because they thought interview and presentation skills would help them in seeking employment in the future.

The relative neglect of listening and speaking skills in FC/ENG101 has been a perpetual concern of teachers since the beginning. By revealing that students vastly felt likewise, this HEQEP-funded needs analysis legitimized such ongoing concerns and brought them to the forefront of teachers' attention. This resulted in a major reform of the English 101 assessment system. From 2012, 15% of the total course points, that is, half of the mid-term points, were allotted to assessment of listening (10%) and speaking (5%). This was a minor change, nonetheless a solid start. Teachers involved in English 101 continued to discuss how listening and speaking could be emphasized further. One suggestion was to divide English 101 into two separate courses, one on reading and writing, and the other on listening and speaking, a possibility likely to materialize in the next academic year in 2014. The needs analyses also confirmed the instructors' views that students of the English Department found certain units in *Advancing English Skills* too simple and therefore dull. In the interviews conducted as part of this study, three teachers, all authors of the upcoming revised edition of *Advancing English Skills*, explained that the units that were regarded as dull were to be dropped in favour of units on more culturally familiar themes such as Bangladeshi food, culture, sports etcetera, which students would hopefully find more engaging. In addition, more group work has now been incorporated, and there are sections on listening and speaking as well as reading and writing. The authors are also considering ways in which English 101 could help students with their other discipline-specific units in the English Department, such as advanced composition and literature later in the course of their studies.

However, not all suggestions gathered through the needs analysis were equally helpful. For example, one instructor working on the revision of *Advancing English Skills* reported that, perhaps in keeping with the expectations of English courses from the primary and secondary levels, a large number of students argued that the English 101 textbook should contain plenty of grammar exercises. Though instructors over recent years have been using Murphy's Intermediate English Grammar to complement *Advancing English Skills*, additional grammar exercises were being included in the revised edition of the English 101 textbook, although the usefulness of such isolated grammar exercises to improve the students' proficiency in English is doubtful.

While such needs analyses can be a useful tool for textbook and syllabus reform, since critical pedagogy is not yet practised at any level, students – and even teachers – cannot propose significant changes to the way that EAP courses function. Without the participants' ability to consider alternatives, needs analysis becomes only a limited tool for bringing about change. Not only should needs analyses be carried out on a regular basis, not just as part of a single project, but training of the student-participants can also go a long way in making the results of needs analyses more effective. A critical-pragmatic approach can prove useful here; through critical interrogation learners will be provided with opportunities to challenge oppressive conventions and imagine alternatives, while pragmatic training can help them adapt to constraints where and when necessary.

Meanwhile, work on the next edition of *Advancing English Skills* continues taking into account the needs of current students. The authors feel that the units could be better written if they had more time to work on the book, while an increased budgetary allocation is necessary to make the book colourful and attractive. They would also like to publish an accompanying book for instructors, which probably will not be possible due to the aforementioned constraints. Yet the authors are hopeful that with a few more modifications, they can create a book which can be used to teach EAP not only in the English Department at Dhaka University, but also across various departments at DU and other public and private universities, as well as in affiliated colleges under the National University in Bangladesh.

CONCLUSION

Hyland and Hamp-Lyons (2002, p. 2) have shown how EAP originated from the broader field of ESP, committed to facilitating a "new kind of literacy," tailoring instruction grounded in an understanding of the cognitive, social, and linguistic demands of specific academic disciplines. Such genesis from ESP has meant that EAP has been characterized by an emphasis on how learners can gain control over strong disciplinary language. However, EAP has also inherited some of ESP's much discussed limitations, in particular, a tendency to work for rather than with subject specialists, to the extent sometimes as to overlook students' cultures, and "a reluctance to critically engage with the values of institutional goals and practices" (Hyland & Hamp-Lyons, 2002, p. 3).

Hamp-Lyons (2001) argues for the need to see needs analysis as a fundamental step to an EAP approach to course design and teaching. It is one of the most effective means of identifying the specific skills set, texts, linguistic forms, and communicative practices that a defined group of learners is considered to be in need of acquiring. By identifying elements of target English situations and using them as the basis of EAP instruction, teachers are able to provide students with the specific language they need to succeed in their courses and future careers, which in turn facilitates learner autonomy.

However, the fluid and amorphous nature of needs analysis makes it a highly complex undertaking. How elements of an EAP setting are identified and defined depends largely on the analyst's own ideology (Robinson, 1991, in Benesch, 1996). While some observers will focus on what learners need to do to perform well, others will be on the lookout for scope for possibilities for change. Benesch (1996) offers the variant of critical needs analysis as the practice of considering a target situation as a site of possible reform by taking into account the hierarchical nature of social institutions. Such an approach also treats as a central concern institutional inequality both inside and outside the institution. Critical needs analysis therefore acknowledges existing structures and instruments of power relations while searching for possible areas of change (Benesch, 1996).

In relation to the FC, Chowdhury (2003) pushed for the need to conduct systematic and periodical/ongoing needs analyses for setting goals to identify students' needs, wants, and expectations. He cautioned, though, that any success was dependent on training the learners first before the feasibility of needs analyses in the context of Dhaka University could be focussed on. In the context of FC, needs analysis has historically failed to include any discussion on empowering the students. As Fairclough (1992) advocates, the need for teachers is to go beyond just thinking critically and reflectively on their pedagogical practicalities and reflect instead on how to help students become critical learners. Learners need to be supported in becoming gradually more autonomous. Learner training would put emphasis on the specific needs of the students and free them from the traditional pedagogical limitations.

It is imperative that teachers synthesise the critical and pragmatic in EAP practice. As discussed, the critical-pragmatic approach to EAP recognises the significant impact of students' exposure to the norms of dominant discourses/conventions and offers a conducive channel in fostering individual learners' needs by making available freedom of choice. Such an approach will allow FC students to not only do well in their studies but also question the curriculum and pedagogy of ENG 101. In practice, then, this means that teachers need to make the "subtle adjustments to practice" (Allison, 1996, p. 99) and move towards a CEAP approach, which will facilitate perpetual questioning of practice while also encouraging students to consider rejecting normative practices.

Teacher training/mentoring programmes have often failed to include in their curriculum and teaching agenda those individuals most concerned with and affected by what teachers know and do. Despite greater emphasis on needs analysis in recent years, as yet in the FC there is no discussion on empowering the learner, and teachers are often theoretically stuck between the paradox of respecting the learner's idiosyncratic needs on one hand and on the other hand calling for "educating" the learner to know their needs. It is time to move beyond the discourse of being complacent about the pragmatism of critical needs analysis and shift towards an environment that fosters critical EAP. As Benesch (2001) has shown, this can be done through rights analysis – a framework that enables the study of power relations in educational settings to disturb and disrupt accepted forms of practice rather than reinforcing conformity. Such a framework will help raise our critical awareness of how language works in relation to how it supports institutional inequalities and allow empowerment of students.

REFERENCES

Allison, D. (1996). Pragmatist discourse and English for academic purposes. *English for Specific Purposes, 15*(2), 85-103.

Bangladesh Bureau of Statistics. (2012). *Bangladesh population and housing census 2011: Socio-economic and demographic report.* Bangladesh: Government of the People's Republic of Bangladesh Retrieved from http://www.bbs.gov.bd/WebTestApplication/userfiles/Image/BBS/Socio_Economic.pdf.

Benesch, S. (1993). ESL, ideology, and the politics of pragmatism. *TESOL Quarterly, 27*(4), 705-717.

Benesch, S. (1996). Needs analysis and curriculum development in EAP: An example of a critical approach. *TESOL Quarterly, 30*(4), 723-738.

Benesch, S. (2001). *Critical English for academic purposes: Theory, politics and practice.* London: Lawrence Erlbaum.

Benesch, S. (2009). Theorizing and practicing critical English for academic purposes. *Journal of English for Academic Purposes. 8*(2), 81-85.

Chaudhury, T. A. (2011). Identifying the English language needs of humanities students at Dhaka University. *Dhaka University Journal of Linguistics, 2*(4), 59-91.

Chowdhury, R. (2003). International TESOL training and EFL contexts: The cultural disillusionment factor. *Australian Journal of Education, 47*(3), 283-302.

Chowdhury, R., & Farooqui, S. (2011). Teacher training and teaching practice: The changing landscape of ELT in secondary education in Bangladesh. In L. Farrell, U. N. Singh, & R. A. Giri (Eds.), *English language education in South Asia: From policy to pedagogy* (pp. 147-159). Delhi, India: Cambridge University Press.

Chowdhury, R., & Kabir, A. H. (forthcoming). Language wars: English education policy and practice in Bangladesh. In R. Kirkpatrick (Ed.), *English education policy in Asia and the Middle East*: Springer.

Chowdhury, R., & Le Ha, P. (2008). Towards locally sensitive and meaningful pedagogy in ELT: Bangladeshi perspectives. *Asia Pacific Journal of Education, 28*(3), 305-316.

Crosling, G., & Ward, I. (2002). Oral communication: The workplace needs and uses of business graduate employees. *English for Specific Purposes, 21*(1), 41-57.

Evans, S. (2010). Business as usual: The use of English in the professional world in Hong Kong. *English for Specific Purposes, 29*(3), 153-167.

Fairclough, N. (1992). Introduction. In N. Fairclough (Ed.), *Critical language awareness* (pp. 1-30). London: Longman.

Flowerdew, J., & Peacock, M. (2001). A preliminary perspective. In J. Flowerdew & M. Peacock (Eds.), *Research perspectives on English for academic purposes* (pp. 8-24). Cambridge, UK: Cambridge University Press.

Hall, G. (2000) Local approaches to critical pedagogy: An investigation into the dilemmas raised by critical approaches to ELT. Lancaster University, Lancaster, UK: Centre for Research in Language Education.

Hamid, O. (2000). A time befitting curricular innovation. *The Dhaka University Studies, 54*(3), 44-57.

Hamp-Lyons, L. (2001). English for academic purposes. In D. Nunan & R. Carter (Eds.), *The Cambridge guide to teaching English to speakers of other languages* (pp. 126-130). Cambridge, UK: Cambridge University Press.

Harwood, N., & Hadley, G. (2004). Demystifying institutional practices: Critical pragmatism and the teaching of academic writing. *English for Specific Purposes, 23*(4), 355-377.

Hasan, M. K. (2004). *A linguistic study of English language curriculum at the secondary level in Bangladesh: A communicative approach to curriculum development.* (PhD), Aligarh Muslim University, Language in India. Retrieved from http://www.languageinindia.com/aug2004/hasandissertation1.html#preface

Hu, G. (2005). English language education in China: Policies, progress, and problems. *Language Policy, 4*(1), 5-24.

Hua, T.-L., & Beverton, S. (2013). General or vocational English courses for Taiwanese students in vocational high schools? Students' perceptions of their English courses and their relevance to their future career. *Educational Research for Policy and Practice, 12*(2), 101-120.

Hyland, K., & Hamp-Lyons, L. (2002). EAP: Issues and directions. *Journal of English for Academic Purposes, 1*(1), 1-12.

Ivanič, R. (1998). *Writing and identity: The discoursal construction of identity in academic writing.* Amsterdam: John Benjamins.

Johns, A. M. (1993). Reading and writing tasks in English for academic purposes classes: Products, processes, and resources. In J. G. Carson & I. Leki (Eds.), *Reading in the composition classroom: Second language perspectives* (pp. 274-289). Boston, MA: Heinle and Heinle.

Kassim, H., & Ali, F. (2010). English communicative events and skills needed at the workplace: Feedback from the industry. *English for Specific Purposes, 29*(3), 168-182.

Khan, R. (2000). The English foundation course at Dhaka University: An evaluation. *The Dhaka University Studies, 57*(1), 77-110.

Langan, J. (2012). *English skills with readings* (8th ed.). New York: McGraw-Hill.

Lobo, A., & Gurney, L. (2013). What did they expect? Exploring a link between students' expectations, attendance and attrition on English language enhancement courses. *Journal of Further and Higher Education*, Advance online publication. doi: 10.1080/0309877X.2013.817002

Murphy, R. (2007). *Intermediate English grammar: Reference and practice for South Asian students* (Second ed.). New Delhi, India: Cambridge University Press.

Pennycook, A. (1990). Critical pedagogy and second language education. *System, 18*(3), 303-314.

Pennycook, A. (1994a). Beyond (f) utilitarianism: English as academic purpose. *Hong Kong Papers in Linguistics and Language Teaching, 17*(1), 13-23.

Pennycook, A. (1994b). *The cultural politics of English as an international language.* London: Longman.

Philpot, S., Curnick, L., Pathare, E., Pathare, G., & Harrison, R. (2011). *Headway academic skills: Reading, writing and study skills.* Oxford, UK: Oxford University Press.

Swales, J. M. (1990). *Genre analysis: English in academic and research settings.* Cambridge, UK: Cambridge University Press.

Raqib Chowdhury
Faculty of Education
Monash University
Melbourne, Australia

Munasir Kamal
Department of English
University of Dhaka
Dhaka, Bangladesh

SURESH CANAGARAJAH

7. EAP IN ASIA

Challenges and Possibilities

INTRODUCTION

Tensions in teaching English for Academic Purposes (EAP) in Asia are related largely to the different ways knowledge construction and academic communication work in Asia and in the West. These tensions are not unique to Asia. Research shows that there are tensions between local and global orientations to academic practices and communication everywhere, even in the West (see Canagarajah, 2002; Lillis & Curry, 2010). The postmodern orientation to knowledge, giving importance to values, ideologies, and identities in knowledge making and disseminating enterprises, has made us sensitive to the tensions in representing local knowledge (from classrooms and communities, for example) in disciplinary discourses. Whereas teachers in Asia may not have addressed these tensions effectively in the past, the postmodern orientation provides avenues for developing new pedagogical orientations for practising an EAP that creatively merges local and global concerns. I write this article from the perspective of teaching EAP in the University of Jaffna (UJ, hereafter), Sri Lanka, where I also served as the head of the English Language Teaching Centre which administered the EAP program.

THE CHALLENGES

I describe a set of interrelated tensions, spanning broad areas of knowledge traditions and extending to pedagogical needs and priorities. Before I explore these tensions in the context of local ecologies of communication and knowledge, it is necessary to stress their importance for EAP. Though one might say that English administrators can design any curricular and pedagogical priorities based on the latest research information or pedagogical trends, students (and teachers) are influenced by practices of knowledge construction and academic communication outside the EAP classroom. The field of language socialization emphasizes that the informal, everyday, and social acquisitions of language and discourse are as important as, or even more important than, what transpires inside classrooms (Duff, 2010). More importantly, influences from outside the English class, including other courses in local languages and academic events in local universities, begin to shape EAP curricular and pedagogical practices as well. Therefore, we cannot ignore tensions of this nature.

I. Liyanage & T. Walker (eds.), English for Academic Purposes (EAP) in Asia, 93–102.
© *2014 Sense Publishers. All rights reserved.*

Orientation to Knowledge

Many local communities have well-established traditions of knowledge construction that differ from Western orientations in the enlightenment/modernist tradition (see chapter by Gunawardena & Petraki, this volume). Research institutions and academic journals in elite universities in the West are still considerably influenced by empirical traditions, despite the emerging deviations from earlier versions of positivistic inquiry. In the traditionally Hindu community where UJ is located, I found considerable variations from this modernist orientation to knowledge. I provide an ethnography of the academic culture in this university in an earlier publication, *Geopolitics of Academic Writing* (Canagarajah, 2002), from which I provide examples below. It is not that local scholars always adopt a tradition-conforming, spiritualist orientation to knowledge, with personal experience and authoritative community texts treated as their main evidence. Their orientation to knowledge is mixed. It is a hybrid of both scientific/empirical and religious/traditional influences. I present in my book the complex ways in which both traditions can inform the same talk or text. For example, a scholar might make a case for the greatness of a Hindu savant and his special divine perception on the basis of empirical evidence in a seminar or article. Even scholars who had obtained doctorates in the West adopted epistemological orientations which were influenced by local traditions after they returned to Sri Lanka. Students who attend these seminars and lectures are influenced by such hybrid orientations to academic discourse.

Some may argue that such a mix of epistemologies may not be persuasive in article submissions or grant applications outside the local community. However, this hybridity does not have to be always disempowering or conflicting. Local orientations can provide a critical vantage point in some cases. I have given examples of how canonical theoretical texts (for example, those of poststructuralist theorists such as Derrida or Foucault) might be read differently in the local context, as scholars resituate the text in their own social conditions and cultural values. I have myself benefited from different orientations to language norms, pedagogies, and literacies from the vantage point of local practices. For example, the plurilingual nature of language contact and communication in local life (much celebrated in pre-colonial local literatures and treatises) made me rethink orientations to monolingual ideologies in English and English-language teaching (see Canagarajah, 2013). However, in some cases, local teachers are uneasy about addressing these tensions. English teachers may also treat the knowledge traditions that inform the disciplinary discourses they teach in EAP as normative and fail to resolve the possible tensions.

Academic Culture

The way local academic cultures function is also different. On the basis of my ethnography, I characterize the local academic culture the following way. The local academic community is:

- more a reading community than a writing community in its literate practices;
- more an oral community than a literate community in its dominant modes of knowledge construction and communicative conventions;
- more a teaching community than a research community;
- a hybrid community which accommodates influences from both the centre and the periphery in its scholarly activity, institutional policies, and literacy practices;
- a civic-minded community that earns its status and sustenance by serving the society;
- a loosely constituted community that accommodates members and institutions of the wider society in its scholarly activities (Canagarajah, 2002, pp. 183-200).

The literacy practices in the local academic community are very different from those in the West. Since there is no strong pressure to publish in prestigious journals for tenure and promotion, local scholars do not spend much time in writing. But they are voracious readers. In fact, their reading spans beyond the narrow boundaries of their field. In this sense, they are very multidisciplinary in their orientation. Their knowledge production occurs mostly in oral interactions rather than in writing. Significant theorization takes place in small discussion circles and more formal academic seminars. Furthermore, local scholars adopt a very functional and pragmatic ethos. As state-funded professionals in public universities, they are expected to put their knowledge to practical use. Therefore, teaching gains much importance. The writers are also always open to consultation by local social institutions and schools on development projects. These features of their academic culture also add to their hybridity in knowledge construction (as discussed above). They keep themselves open to interactions with the non-academic community. Their scholarship is made accessible to those outside the university. In all these senses, they resemble public intellectuals in the West. It is not specialization in narrow areas of disciplinary issues that matters (as in elite universities in the West), but the ability to relate their scholarship to community concerns and interest.

How does this academic culture affect EAP? It is possible that teachers and students in EAP courses adopt broader orientations to disciplinary texts. For example, they might interpret the texts outside strictly disciplinary constructs. They might relate the texts to their social and community concerns. In both the local academic culture and EAP pedagogies, this orientation to texts is influenced by the lack of access to the conversations and publications of western academic communities, resulting in a disconnect. Since the contexts and discourses that motivate the texts are not accessible to local students, scholars, and teachers, they may adopt styles of interpretation and meanings that are local.

Literate Genres

For the reasons given above, the styles of writing locally are also considerably different from academic texts in the West. Academic articles can be very hybrid, with a mix of personal voice, narrative structure, digressions, and social applications. Articles published in local academic journals can thus be very different from the data-driven articles in the West. In addition to the local preference for more expressive and engaged voices, deriving from local epistemologies, these differences also result from material conditions. Since local scholars do not have access to the latest academic publications, they do not perform an extensive literature review to frame their articles. They might simply announce their research questions and proceed to discussing their data, as I have illustrated from articles they have published even in the West (see Canagarajah, 2002). For the same reason, they may also frame the significance and rationale for their study in terms of local community concerns (which I label a "civic ethos") and not in terms of new knowledge. Moreover, local articles may adopt a style of indirection, in keeping with what I call a "humility ethos" that requires that a scholar humble him/herself in the presence of other scholars. All these tendencies will result in an article deviating considerably from the canonical opening of an academic article, which Swales (1990), in his influential Create a Research Space (CARS) model, characterizes as made up of explicit framing in relation to prior knowledge in the discipline to identify a gap in the disciplinary conversation and showing how the article occupies the gap. There are other non-discursive differences as well. Local journals may not have a uniform style manual for citations. Even within the same article, scholars may adopt different citation conventions Local scholars adopt a pragmatic orientation that sufficient clues to trace the publication are adequate in citations.

We can guess the implications for EAP from literate genres of this nature. Local teachers of English may face tensions between the data-driven and explicit text structures of the West and the more indirect and conversational writing styles locally. Students also have to navigate both kinds of texts in their content-level courses.

Language Norms

There are also tensions in language norms that local teachers and students encounter in EAP (see chapters by Kafle, and Ashraf, Hakim, & Zulfiqar, this volume). It must be recognized that in many Asian universities most content-based instruction is in the vernacular (Tamil in the case of UJ). There are a few optional tracks (such as in Science or Business in UJ) in which students can choose to do the entire degree in the English medium. In this context, it is important to ask whether a pedagogy for academic purposes in English has any local relevance. It is possible to argue that EAP has to be taught to local students in order for professional communication which might require English after graduation or to proceed to graduate level education in the West. In either case, the students in EAP courses will be mindful of academic communication in Tamil in their content-level classes.

Another language norm to contend with is the fairly well-established Sri Lankan English that differs from prestige varieties of British or American English. The English used by scholars and professionals in local writing and oral communication in English interactions is considerably indigenized. Should EAP then be taught in local or prestige varieties of English for students? Whereas teachers may use materials from the West in prestige varieties for instruction in their classes, students will find academic communication outside their classes in Tamil or Sri Lankan English. Even those students who do content-level courses in English will face tensions between local varieties of English and prestige varieties in their classes.

Communicative Skills

The fact that instruction in content courses in most universities is in the vernacular does not mean that there are no uses of English for these students. What we found in UJ was that students needed English for reading reference materials. Since scholarly books are difficult to find in Tamil, as there is no extensive market for academic books at advanced/specialized levels, and few publishers for such works, content-based instructors refer their students to books published in English. Similarly, instructors do their reading in English in order to prepare their lectures in Tamil. Those who lack proficiency in English are therefore handicapped when they go to the library for reference reading. This realization motivates EAP instructors in UJ to focus mostly on reading proficiency in English. Such a course would focus on teaching students the specialized vocabulary, registers, and grammatical structures in their areas of study. Also, the genre conventions of typical scholarly writing in the field will be taught. However, such a focus creates a dilemma. Instructors are caught between the contrasting pulls of teaching reading skills for local academic purposes and teaching integrated skills for study and work abroad (see chapter by Liyanage & Walker, this volume). For example, when students apply for graduate study in foreign universities, they require skills of writing application letters and passing tests such as Graduate Records Examination (GRE) which may need writing and listening. Later, they might engage in advanced writing, speaking, and integrated skills when they follow graduate level courses abroad.

Teaching Practices

As we proceed further to the pedagogical options for teachers in EAP courses, there are other dilemmas between locally valued practices and global trends (see chapters by Chowdhury & Kamal and Gao & Bartlett, this volume). Outside Asia, especially in the West, EAP is moving towards more practice-based and collaborative orientations, influenced by approaches of language socialization (see Duff, 2010). Teachers and researchers realize that product-oriented teaching of vocabulary, registers, grammatical structures, and genre conventions is inadequate for many reasons. Students need communicative competence in these contexts. Influenced by models such as communities of practice and legitimate peripheral participation (Wenger, 1998), scholars realize that students have to be inducted gradually into academic discourses to become insiders to those disciplinary communities, understanding the nuances of usage that mark successful practice. Also, proficiency in form is useless without the values and epistemologies that inform these communicative genres. For this purpose, teachers provide real-life tasks and activities, while also encouraging students to participate in academic events and communication, in order to gain socialization into disciplinary communities. However, teachers in local universities tend to be more product oriented. Models such as communities of practice are still new to many teachers in UJ. Often they do not have the resources to design tasks and activities by themselves. In most cases, EAP instructors resort to taking sample texts of that discipline (i.e., geography or biology) to class and providing comprehension exercises to students.

POSSIBILITIES

It is clear that there are some significant dilemmas in EAP teaching in Asian universities. While some of these dilemmas result from serious philosophical and communicative differences, others result from lack of access and resources. However, there are ways in which local universities can negotiate these challenges to construct more relevant and meaningful pedagogies. These pedagogies may not only help local students succeed in both local and international contexts, they can also help reconfigure knowledge representation and academic communication in general. Before I outline such an approach, I will review some emerging realizations that motivate such new EAP pedagogies.

Orientations to Knowledge Construction

The backlash against positivist orientations to knowledge in the postmodern context has encouraged new orientations to inquiry. Even in the West, there is a feeling that more qualitative, personal, holistic, and ethical forms of research have been overlooked. The focus on objectivity and controlled experimentation has resulted in the ignoring of diverse other ways of knowing. Approaches such as autoethnography, narrative studies, and action research, becoming popular in diverse areas of social, educational, and communicative sciences, adopt personal and situated forms of knowing (see Canagarajah, 1996). These developments have encouraged scholars from non-Western communities to make a case for their own forms of knowing. Tuhiwai-Smith (1999), for example, critiqued Western positivistic forms of inquiry for suppressing indigenous forms of knowledge and concerns. Others have critiqued the unequal relationship between the researcher and the researched – that is, often it is a case of researchers from (Western) privileged communities doing research on subaltern communities. This inequality leads to researchers from outside communities constructing knowledge relating to local communities. I have described how such inequalities in knowledge production affect disciplinary discourses relating to Asian contexts (Canagarajah, 2002).

There is now a readiness to accommodate intellectual and scholarly orientations that are more diverse in the academic community. There is more openness to mixed methods or hybrid approaches to inquiry in research. We read also of studies based on traditions of knowledge and inquiry in local communities. De Souza (2002) discusses how he had to adopt local epistemologies and rituals of the Kashinawa indigenous community in Brazil to understand their literacy practices. There are also scientific explorations into local cultural traditions and knowledge constructs. For example, the American federal institution, National Institutes for Health, is doing research on Asian traditions of alternative medicine to tap into their potential (see Canagarajah, 2002).

Findings from Language Socialization

Scholars in language socialization are increasingly finding that academic genres are difficult to define in bounded and discrete terms. Reviewing studies on academic socialization, Duff (2008, 2010) points out that academic genres are blurred and hybrid. For example, she finds that academic lectures mix scholarly citations and references to popular culture. They may contain multiple genres within them, such as dialogue and narrative. The same applies to written genres. The notion that disciplinary writing is impersonal, jargon ridden, and data driven is not always true. In many disciplines, we are beginning to see articles that accommodate the personal voice, narrative, and a conversational flow. There are more radical experimentations with writing in the humanities and social sciences. Scholars are composing alternate forms of research reporting that would better reflect our emerging realizations on the nature of research and knowledge production. These are polyphonous or dialogic texts that encode multiple voices/ perspectives simultaneously and engage the reader more actively in the interpretive process. These texts invoke developments in new ways of reading and writing in postmodern literature. Marcus and Fischer (1986) refer to experimental texts in their field of anthropology as *modernist ethnographies* (to contrast with traditional realist ethnographies), while some composition scholars call their new genres *multivocal* texts (see Cushman, 1996).

Scholars of disciplinary socialization also find that multilingual scholars who shuttle between the languages and discourses of the local and the global adopt a critical and resistant orientation to disciplinary expectations. In the fashion of the nexus of multimembership in the communities of practice orientation (see Wenger, 1998), they bring influences from their local communities to inform their academic practices and communication. Rather than being unsuccessful, these creative insertions of local values and knowledge provide a strategic edge for multilingual scholars. They are able to bring new insights into dominant disciplinary conversations and initiate new inquiry. These studies show that disciplinary socialization does not have to be one sided. Local scholars can creatively draw from their own resources and values to address mainstream disciplinary discourses.

I have elsewhere reported the writing practice of a senior scholar from UJ who shuttles between languages and communities in his publications (Canagarajah,

99

2006b). In analyzing his English writing for local and Western audiences (in journals published in Sri Lanka and Sweden, respectively), I show how the scholar adopts norms and conventions that are valued by the respective audiences. In other words, while he uses more Sri Lankan English, personal voice, and narrative voice in the Sri Lankan journal, he shifts to greater objectivity and formality in the Western journal. However, he does not do this one-sidedly. He also brings a greater sense of objectivity than is usually warranted to the local journal and greater personal voice and local stand point to the Western journal. In drawing from alternate scholarly traditions, he manages to insert something original and critical in his writing for the respective audiences. In other words, he uses his multilingualism and multiculturalism as a resource to both shuttle between communities fluidly and also provide a critical edge to his writing.

Insights from Academic Literacies

Writing practices and communicative conventions of this nature have generated a debate in circles of academic literacies on how to instruct novice scholars and students effectively. With the focus on products of academic communication proving useless, scholars are moving towards more practice-based instructional approaches (Lillis & Scott, 2007). They realize that teaching the language structures and conventions are ineffective when genres are blurred and hybrid. Furthermore, in a context when students and scholars have to shuttle between different languages and knowledge traditions in a global educational context, they are exploring other approaches. The new realization is that we have to focus on more subtle competencies such as language awareness, negotiation strategies, and discourse practices. In other words, students should develop an awareness of language norms and genre conventions in different contexts. They have to appreciate that these norms and conventions are connected to diverse cultures and traditions, and that it is important to engage with audience expectations for successful uptake of academic communication. To shuttle between varying norms, they have to develop diverse negotiation strategies. They have to learn how to shift their interpretive or writing approaches for different communities. More importantly, they have to also know where and when to deviate from local norms, in the light of the other resources and values they bring with them, in an effort to make spaces for their own voices and perspectives in academic communication. Such an orientation encourages a practice-based orientation to discourse and learning. It is not simply knowing the norms and conventions that helps; one has to know how to deploy, renegotiate, and reconfigure norms strategically in different contexts to be successful (see Canagarajah, 2006a, for an elaboration of this pedagogy in writing studies).

CONCLUSION

These developments point to a different agenda for EAP in Asia. They suggest ways in which local teachers can resolve their dilemmas for a productive pedagogy. If teachers can conceive of EAP as enabling students to merge their competing cultural, academic, and linguistic traditions, they do not have to compartmentalize learning to local and global domains. Teachers and students do not have to be torn between orientating to global norms and suppressing the local values, or practising local norms while professing adherence to global discourses and conventions. They have to recognize that engaging with dominant conventions from the standpoint of one's local traditions and values can lead to successful academic communication. In fact, such a practice of negotiation and appropriation can lead to critical academic communication that can provide a strategic edge to local students. To accomplish this orientation, teachers can bring to the EAP classroom texts from local academic cultures in the vernacular as well. As students shuttle between local and Western academic literacies, they will develop the awareness and strategies to navigate competing academic traditions. In this manner, teachers can encourage students to participate in local academic events in the vernacular and/or draw from their content-based instruction in the vernacular to inform their EAP instruction. Appreciating the differences between local and Western communicative conventions will help students to not only develop proficiency in English communication, but also understand the rationale behind local conventions. This approach would also help local teachers deal with the lack of access to materials and resources for EAP. By tapping into both English and vernacular texts and events of academic communication in local communities, teachers can develop the awareness for students to shuttle between different communicative contexts. In other words, this would be a pedagogy of academic multilingualism. Teaching for academic purposes will not be compartmentalized according to different languages or communities. The pedagogy can address the competencies required for diverse communities when students shuttle between them, while drawing from the hybrid values and resources they bring with them.

I have broadly outlined a pedagogy that we need to develop more programmatically in the future. What I provide is an argument for dealing with the tensions and dilemmas in EAP more honestly and directly. Local traditions and norms can be resources that can be used to our advantage, and not something to be embarrassed about.

REFERENCES

Canagarajah, A. S. (1996). From critical research practice to critical research reporting. *TESOL Quarterly, 30*(2), 321-330.

Canagarajah, A. S. (2002). *A geopolitics of academic writing*. Pittsburgh, PA: University of Pittsburgh Press.

Canagarajah, A. S. (2006a). The place of World Englishes in composition: Pluralization continued. *College Composition and Communication, 57*(2), 586-619.

Canagarajah, A. S. (2006b). Toward a writing pedagogy of shuttling between languages: Learning from multilingual writers. *College English, 68*(6), 589-604.

Canagarajah, A. S. (2013). *Translingual practice: Global Englishes and cosmopolitan relations*. New York: Routledge.

Cushman, E. (1996). The rhetorician as an agent of social change. *College Composition and Communication, 47*(1), 7-28.

de Souza, L. M. (2002). A case among cases, a world among worlds: The ecology of writing among the Kashinawa in Brazil. *Journal of Language, Identity, and Education, 1*(4), 261-278.

Duff, P. A. (2008). Language socialization, higher education, and work. In P. A. Duff & N. Hornberger (Eds.), *Encyclopedia of language and education* (Vol. 8: Language socialization, pp. 257-270). Boston, MA: Springer.

Duff, P. A. (2010). Language socialization into academic discourse communities. *Annual Review of Applied Linguistics, 30*(1), 169-192.

Lillis, T., & Curry, M. J. (2010). *Academic writing in a global context: The politics and practices of publishing in English.* London: Routledge.

Lillis, T., & Scott, M. (2007). Defining academic literacies research: Issues of epistemology, ideology and strategy. *Journal of Applied Linguistics, 4*(1), 5-32.

Marcus, G. E., & Fischer, M. M. (1986). *Anthropology as cultural critique: An experimental moment in the human sciences.* Chicago, IL: University of Chicago Press.

Swales, J. M. (1990). *Genre analysis: English in academic and research settings.* Cambridge, UK: Cambridge University Press.

Tuhiwai-Smith, L. (1999). *Decolonizing methodologies: Research and indigenous peoples.* London: Zed Books.

Wenger, E. (1998). *Communities of practice.* Cambridge, UK: Cambridge University Press.

Suresh Canagarajah
Departments of Applied Linguistics and English
Pennsylvania State University
USA

SUBJECT INDEX

SUBJECT INDEX

Lightning Source UK Ltd.
Milton Keynes UK
UKOW04f2118081014

239843UK00009B/841/P